The Art of the Struggle

Reggie Flowers

MANIFOLD GRACE
Publishing House LLC

The Art of the Struggle
Copyright © 2016 Reggie Flowers

Cover Art and Design: Adam Macri

ISBN: 978-1-937400-70-5
ISBN: 978-1-937400-71-2 (eBook)

Printed in the United States of America

Published by Manifold Grace Publishing House, LLC
Southfield, Michigan 48033
www.manifoldgracepublishinghouse.com

Dedication

I dedicate this book to my lovely wife and three children. Christine, your invaluable perspective, love, support and encouragement helped me throughout this entire journey. I am forever grateful for your patience during the rough times and I look forward to a life worthy of continuous celebration together.

Brielle, RJ, and Alex - you have been my internal driving force for accomplishing my goals. My goals have been centered around your futures and working to ensure each of you live an incredible and blessed life. Love each and every one of you.

Acknowledgments

Mom, thank you for everything. There isn't enough room on this page for me to share each and every thing I'm thankful for. You have been by my side through this entire process. From childhood to manhood, you have always encouraged me to believe I am special, blessed, and will be a blessing to those around me. Thank you for giving everything you had with no expectations. I love you very much.

My mother-in-law, Gladys, who kept the family lifted up in prayer, cared for our children and never lost faith. Thank you!

Thanks to my family who did their part to help me get to this moment. I am very grateful for each of you.

Contents

Introduction

Progress is essential to your happiness and wellbeing. It's one of the most gratifying emotions one can experience in a lifetime. Progress fuels desire. It suggests increase. It yearns for excitement. It attracts possibility. Progress encourages you to take on your next journey. It aids in your ability to feel as though everything you've sacrificed thus far was worth it. Progress is a required need of mankind. Investing time wisely becomes a priority to you. Ultimately, you have never felt more alive than you do when you're in the presence of progress. We all have the potential to experience progress consistently in our lives. Progress isn't just given to those who desire it; it's given to those who deserve it.

What about *regress*? It is an opposing force of progress. When the markets crashed in 2008, millions of Americans were economically devastated. People, for the first time, found themselves unwillingly becoming regressive. 401Ks were reduced to 200.5Ks. Property values were significantly depreciated. Foreclosures were at an all-time high. When someone said job security in conversation, people would listen with anticipation for the punch line. This era validated the deconstruction of the American Dream. You and I were told to go to school, get an education, and find a great job. This was a strategy for long term job, and retirement; security.

Millions were dumbfounded. They couldn't understand why they were being penalized for obedience. The hard-working couple that bought a home in the right community and saved their money or the single mother who worked two or three jobs to put herself through night school and graduate college; couldn't understand. "The struggle is real" is a phrase that has now become a statement that described the experiences of millions.

Either you are moving forward or you are going backwards, what you are not doing is standing still. I think we both can agree; no one wants to experience constant defeats or failures.

It would be my pleasure to extend an invitation for you to join me on one of the most incredible, figuratively speaking, roller coaster rides from *broke to riches and back to being broke while working back to riches - again.* My ride began just before my 20th birthday. During this time, I was a full-time college student attending Oakland University. I was your typical pre-med biology major, bombarded with coursework and studying which left very little time for a social life. My goal was to become an orthopedic surgeon; I often chuckled when people asked what inspired me to pursue being a doctor?

My answer was quite simple. My mother had two college degrees, so it was expected (demanded) of me to at least get one. I desired to be successful and I was pretty good at math and science so, I'll be a doctor. I went online to do some research and googled the top five earning physicians in the medical field. (Yes it was teenage logic!) If I'm not mistaken, I think orthopedics was either number one or number two. Since I had an athletic background, the concept of working on bones just made sense.

I shadowed physicians at the beginning of my sophomore year and by the end of the year I no longer wanted to be an orthopedic surgeon. What happened? Can you believe some of the doctors were working between 12 to 36 hour shifts? I thought to myself this is crazy, there are only 24 hours in a day and I will be working 36 of them. At this point I knew in my heart of hearts that being an orthopedic surgeon wasn't for me.

Within a matter of weeks after the decision to change my

career path, my mother received a phone call from a stranger out of New York. She had found my mother's contact information online and gave her a call. Keep in mind this was in 2004, personal information wasn't readily available like it is in 2016. Phyllis (the stranger) informed my mother that an article featuring her was on the front page of her local newspaper in New York. At that time my mother was living in the small city of Port Huron, located in Michigan. The local newspaper was just that, a local newspaper. It wasn't clear to my mother, or I, how this article made it to upstate New York.

The article was titled *"Ex-cop, Retired Social Worker Heavily Involved in the Community"*. In the article, my mother was quoted regarding her concerns about Gen Y and millennials being unable to successfully retire with pensions and social security benefits. Phyllis (the New Yorker), felt compelled to reach out and see if my mother was open to an opportunity to earn additional money outside of what she was currently making. My mother explained to Phyllis that she was not interested at the moment, but she told Phyllis that her son was looking for something different.

I remember that Monday evening vividly. I had just returned from the Oakland Center; or the OC which was the hub of student activity; after studying for a biology test. After only being in my dorm room for an hour, this strange number with the 716 area code showed up on my caller ID. Typically I don't take phone calls from numbers I don't recognize, but that evening I was led by Holy Spirit to answer the phone and I did. After small talk, Phyllis asked me to join a presentation call in a couple of hours that evening. She recommended that I try to get someone on this call with me. I immediately called my best friend and told him to join the conference call. He did and we both listened to the presentation that evening. Before the call was even remotely close to being over; something was different. Instinctively I knew that my life would never be the same. Have you ever had that feeling you could not explain, but you knew everything about your life was about to change for the better? That's what happened to me. I felt it deep down in my soul.

The information I received was so inspirational, it was unlike anything I had ever experienced in my life. Feeling overwhelmed with excitement was an understatement. I didn't have any doubts that God was answering a prayer. After my decision to discontinue my pre-med major I had prayed to God seeking direction and clarity.

On the call, I was introduced to two wealth principles: residual income and leveraged income. I also heard testimonies from average people who were making more in one month than they used to earn in an entire year.

After the conference call I got back on the phone with Phyllis and she asked me a series of questions to qualify my interest. I told her that I loved everything I heard and wanted to know more. The only challenge was I didn't have the initial capital to get started. She told me that wasn't a problem, and the next step was to get on the phone with the presenter who happened to be a multimillionaire. This was the first time I'd had the opportunity to speak to a millionaire. I can't deny that I was quite nervous, but Phyllis did such a phenomenal job introducing Mrs. Davis to me. It helped me feel comfortable getting on the phone and speaking with her.

The conversation between Mrs. Davis and I went from a phone introduction to a series of events and has transcended into a lifelong friendship. The events started with me looking for airfare from Michigan to California, which I only had 72 hours to book, all while doing it as your typical financially strapped college student. No job. No income. And definitely, no assets. I had to quickly find and employ a strategy to get the money. So I had to rely on a best-kept secret. The ATM at the bank of Mom. I asked if she would give me the money. For the first time in my life, mom didn't have the extra money to send me to California. Now I'm worried.

As a matter of fact, she suggested that she could send me to Africa for less than California. I called Phyllis back, and with worry evidenced in my voice, told her my dilemma. I distinctly remember her saying this to me, "Boy.... don't call me back until you find a way." Phyllis proceeded to hang up on me. I thought, who does this woman think she is? Then I remembered that she was successful, I was financially broke and she was interested in helping me change my circumstances. I searched online for hours running multiple itinerary scenarios and finally I landed a round-trip flight leaving Detroit International airport and arriving in Santa Ana for $268. Boom! It was on!

THE RISE

I returned from the convention excited and ready to go. My mother was late paying some of her bills to help me get the startup capital. I enrolled immediately as a new distributor. I had a private business reception at my home with 19 of my closest friends and family. That evening 17 of my friends did not feel like this business was for them. I felt slightly discouraged, but I was determined to prove to them that this was what I thought it was.

After being in business for 18 days I was able to recoup my initial investment. By my 30th day, I earned an additional $1700. Over the next year everything seemed to be going well. During this time, I found out that I was going to be the father of a little girl. I found myself very frustrated because I wasn't earning the type of money that would allow me to continue my business full-time and provide for my family. So, I quit. I didn't contact Phyllis or Mrs. Davis, I just left, quietly. I was embarrassed and ashamed. They both believed in me deeply, but my belief in myself dissipated. I think that was the first, and only, time I attempted to give up on my dreams.

Seems like the newspaper always brought me luck, and so my search for a job began. Once again the local newspaper helped me. I found a job as a car salesman. Business at the dealership was going extremely well. I was earning more money than I had ever earned in my life. But, for some reason I didn't feel fulfilled. After being exposed to the opportunity for both time and money freedom, it became hard to accept this job as my best option. So, after a year at the dealership I made a firm decision. THIS IS IT! I'm done working six days a week and 12 hours a day; away from my family. I mustered up the courage to give Mrs. Davis a call and ask her if she would reconsider working with me and she said yes. I returned to my home based business with a vengeance. I put it all on the line, my focus was greater than it had ever been, and I was non-negotiable about success. Within seven months I achieved the first senior position within the company. This positioned me to earn a multi six-figure income. By the eighth month I had generated more than five figures in one month. By the 15th month I was running a seven-figure business. By the time I was 23; I owned and operated a multimillion dollar business with all the benefits and none of the headaches of traditional business.

Everything was like I'd dreamed. I was able to help my mother out financially. I donated to two great causes. I took frequent vacations, sometime as frequently as nine times a year. I was living the dream. My family was no longer struggling emotionally, spiritually, or economically. I was on the fast track to a seven-figure annual income. So many of my colleagues had reached a certain level of success and I knew I wasn't too far behind them. I was traveling all around the country coaching and training thousands of people on personal development and building a successful home based business. I strove for greatness and ultimately became a top producer, globally. This led to assisting my mentor at the convention, training 18 to 20,000 people. I had the honor of being featured on prime-time television. Money was flowing quickly and abundantly every single week. I believed I could take on the world. Little did I know how big the world truly was. There comes a time when you learn that your talent can take you places your character won't keep you.

THE FALL

Typically, things go wrong when there is a consistent error in judgment or strategy. The challenge with "the fall" is, it slowly compounds over time before it exposes itself. At that point it is too late to reverse the outcome. It's kind of like eating candy consistently, over a long period of time, eventually you're going to get cavities. It doesn't happen from the first bag a candy or even the second, however, when you consistently have a bag of candy each week - for 40 weeks straight, it's going to wear down or destroy the enamel that's protecting your teeth.

The candy that happened to ruin my teeth was my growing ego sprinkled with arrogance. It's true, the person it happens to never believes it would happen to them. I was one of 'them'. I thought all the rewards and accolades were because of my greatness. I felt like I had mastered success and taken complete ownership of it. That's where I sadly made my mistake, success cannot be owned. It can only be rented, and each day rent is due. The rotting teeth started with an exorbitant amount of vacations, golf outings, and shopping sprees. I was working less and spending more which is the perfect equation for an emotional and economic catastrophe. Let me tell you, I fell hard; so hard. This round ball hit the ground and exploded. I lost interest in everything, lost focus, fell into debt and spiraled into depression. In the words of my two-year-old "what a mess" I was in. Before I knew it, I was back where I didn't want to be. Face first in the mud of life's jungle.

THE JUNGLE OF THE STRUGGLE

It's ironic: I would have never thought that a guy like me would be subject to struggling. After all, I had a good childhood, a strong mother who loved me a lot and did whatever she could do for me. I was told early on in life that I was special, loved, and would help a lot of people. I believed it. I didn't lack the confidence, courage, or ambition to achieve my dreams. After graduating high school, my vision was clear and concise. I could see all the success that was coming my way. In my mind, it was going to be incredibly easy. Thinking back, never in my wildest imagination would I think that what I went through over the last ten years, would've happened to me. I thought people who struggled usually had low self-esteem, poor morals, or a lack of direction. I soon learned I was dead wrong. Anyone can suffer from this illness and not one human being was safe from being affected by struggle.

While in the *jungle of the struggle*, I made a decision to document my experiences, how they affected me, and what strategies I would use to overcome my challenges. I knew that this information would soon serve and help others. It would have been selfish of me to keep it to myself. Whenever you're going through tough times and experiencing hardships, your solutions will arrive in phases. The key to successfully escaping is your ability to identify and recognize which part of the phase you are in. Once you know where you are, then you can employ the 5 Laws to your benefit.

The jungle is a strengthening exercise full of pain, struggle, and minor defeats. Without personal development, I probably wouldn't have made it out of the jungle successfully. I learned that we become whatever we think about. I had no idea that thoughts were actual things. Therefore, I had to choose my words and sentences carefully. I thought I had a great attitude until I was exposed to real issues and did not know how to cope with my failure. I quickly realized that I did not know nearly as much as I thought I did about life. If I knew as much as I thought I did, I would not be in the jungle of the struggle and could have avoided it altogether. I knew it was going be important for me to focus on growth. Becoming a student of life and a stronger person would equip me to outgrow my problems.

In the midst of the jungle of struggle, I developed The Law of the Five E's:

1. Law of Embracement
2. Law of Engagement
3. Law of Equipping
4. Law of Empowerment
5. Law of Elevation

I moved through each of these phases sequentially. By moving through each phase, I gained a greater ability to effectively surpass my personal struggles. I know that no two struggles are the same and you may be thinking I don't understand, or I haven't experienced what you have. You're right to some degree, but *The Art of the Struggle* provides a universal blueprint that can help you no matter where you are in your struggle. I'm going to teach you how to escape the jungle of the struggle and equip you to live your greater purpose.

The Law of the Five E's will become the pillars upon which your empire stands. There are other fundamental skills that you're going to have to master outside of the Five E's, but these are the building blocks for the other areas you'll need to master.

Get ready. What you are holding in your hand is a comprehensive plan for radical transformation. This isn't just another self-help, inspirational, how-to guide. *The Art of the Struggle* was derived from my very own personal need. As you read, you are going to observe over a decade of refined human potential, coupled with a proven strategy.

The 5 Incontrovertible Laws for Transformation, Achievement and Fulfillment.

Law of Embracement
For transformation to occur you must welcome it:
When something is enjoyable to us we pull it closer, when it's not enjoyable we push it away. You must align yourself with the problems you firmly resent.

Law of Engagement
You must be a part of your own rescue:
The only person responsible for the overall outcome of your life is you. It's your responsibility to make the necessary corrections and changes to live a great life. Your family, friends, and co-workers do not determine your quality of life, only you have that power.

Law of Equipping
You must have the right tools for the right job:
Becoming more than you already are requires new skills. These skills give you access to new possibilities within yourself. Every leader needs to welcome and add new skills to their human toolbox. These skills include:

Vision: Seeing beyond your current circumstances.
Mindset: Strengthening your mental muscle.
Standards: Demanding more of yourself.
Perspective: What's true to you will become your view.

Law of Empowerment
You must fuel progress:
When you obtain new knowledge, skills, and philosophies, the worst thing you can do is not put what you know into action. Empowerment is: what to do + how to do it + why you do it. You must put these new skills to test, evaluate your outcome, and adjust when necessary.

Law of Elevation
Growth impacts everything around you:
When you are intentional about your growth, everyone and everything around you is positively affected.

Law 1: Embracement

For transformation to occur you must welcome it:
When something is enjoyable to us, we pull it closer, when it's not enjoyable we push it away. You must align yourself with the problems you firmly resent.

Disadvantages are merely psychologically limiting beliefs about yourself and the circumstances you've experienced throughout the duration of your life.

Chapter One:

Wonderful Disadvantages

Disadvantages Are to Your Advantage

Let me ask you a question: Why aren't you living the life of your dreams? Think about it. We could all have passion, excitement, and fulfillment. We could have a greater impact on our friends, family, and community if we choose to. So, what prevents us from reaching this lofty goal? Although there are many valid reasons, I found this one to be most consistent. Ready? It's your lack of belief in yourself. How does it happen? It's those two little voices arguing in the back of your head. I refer to one as your "angel" voice and it encourages you. The other voice, the "enemy", discourages you. A majority of people allow the loud voice of the enemy to drown out the angel voice. It does not matter how many books you may have read, seminars you've attended, or affirmations you've said at the top of your lungs – it's not until your beliefs and thoughts are congruent that you will see the change in your life that you are seeking.

In our minds, there is a battle for dominance between the two voices. One voice is saying you can and the other voice is constantly saying you can't. You're stuck in the middle trying to figure out which voice to follow. Because society tells us that having negative feelings or being in a negative environment is normal, we tend to listen to the voice that actually tears us apart. You listen to that voice more because it usually relates to your current situation. Beyond our own thoughts, we have so many voices influencing our lives. We have influences from radio, television, and social media telling us how to look, act, and sound. It becomes harder for us to hear our own inner voice, the voice that's actually authentic and true to ourselves. Your true voice invokes conversations about your wonderful disadvantages.

What's so wonderful about your disadvantages? Disadvantages are like the weights in the gym. They are heavy, hard, and sometimes dangerous, but they are needed to place a greater demand on the mental muscle. Once the mental muscle has been torn, it can begin its reconstructive process. There is short-term pain for long-term gain. If you don't build the mental muscle, there will be long-term pain and short-term gains. Too often, we give the wrong attention to the things we feel are not fair in our lives. What do you perceive as disadvantages in your life? You may feel you had an unfair childhood, your community was lacking, or your parents may not have afforded you the opportunities you believe you deserved.

Disadvantages are merely psychologically limiting beliefs about yourself and circumstances you've experienced throughout the duration of your life. Let's start with money; it happens to be one of the most controversial topics next to religion and politics. Maybe you've been working hard over the past five to ten years. You haven't received an increase in compensation. There's little to no money saved for the future. Trust me, I know the feeling. Most people believe earning more money is the solution to their financial struggles. Logically, this makes sense. And because it makes sense, you believe it to be true. However, if earning more money was the official solution, we wouldn't be familiar with riches to rags stories. I bet you can name at least a half dozen celebrities and athletes that lost it all.

The lack of money isn't the real issue, although it feels like it. The real issue is a poor skill set with money management. It is your disadvantage. There is good news; you can improve this skill set by educating yourself online, through financial mentorship from money experts. There are many experts like Suze Orman and Dave Ramsey that took their financial tragedies, learned from them, and now host top syndicated shows on radio and television about the importance of financial intelligence. Your money is a representation of a specific set of internal values. The way you handle money is based on your values and beliefs about money. When you have a new relationship with money, you will be able to harness its value the correct way.

I had to be real with myself about my lazy, emotional, and disrespectful relationship with money. Money meant very little to me. I often over spent on "stuff" with little or no value. This behavior transcended into my early twenties. The risk became greater because I was earning more income and in return spending more money.

I remember traveling to conventions and checking into the hotel, hoping the payment I made on the credit card before I left home cleared in time. My credit card limit was $600 and the room for three nights totaled $749. This meant I had to be resourceful, but it was very stressful. I started to resent each calendar quarter when it was time to go to convention. That means four times a year I was reminded how bad things were financially.

There were times I would get to the grocery store and before shopping, check my balance. By the time I completed shopping and got to the checkout register, my card was declined. It was unbelievably frustrating. Within the span of an hour some small amount would have gone through and totally changed the dynamics of my balance. There are many more stories I could tell. Going from making a six figure income to barely making ANY money was devastating. Trials like this constantly revealed themselves for five straight years. The lessons learned helped redefine the way I valued and managed money.

Your career, is it a disadvantage? Do you work long hours and find yourself eternally communicating that your job is preventing you from having the time to achieve your dreams? Do you find yourself saying, "If I had a job that only required less hours a week or if I had the weekends off, I would have more time to pursue my dreams?" These are common thoughts and beliefs of ninety-five percent of the global population. Typically, the cup is half full with this group unless you're in the process of transitioning. Working to provide for your family is never a disadvantage. In fact, your job is your advantage. It can help you focus on your goals. It can inspire you to learn new skills. It can motivate you. Motivation is a by-product of two emotions. You can be motivated by inspiration or desperation. Being somewhere you dislike for eight to ten hours a day can give you a strong reason to improve your circumstances.

Ninety-five percent of the population bought the lie that if they had their ideal conditions met, their success would be inevitable. Everyone has 24 hours in a day. The difference between a person getting productive results and a person not getting the results they want is how they use their time. I call this the Law of Discretionary Time. It's not about the time that's already accounted for, it's how your spare time is being invested or spent. Embrace what you can't change and focus your energy on what you have control of. I know you have a lot on your plate. Between family, work and all the awesome distractions, very little time is left to pursue your hearts desires. That statement is accurate; however, five percent of the population faced those same challenges. The difference was their willingness to sacrifice downtime, spare time, and recreational time for a season. In exchange for their sacrifice they are able to see their desires, dreams and goals materialize.

You won't believe how often I hear people use their spouse or significant other as an excuse for the reason they haven't achieved any of their goals or dreams. Leaders in my network marketing organization would tell me that their spouses or loved ones stopped them from taking massive action towards their goals. This is the reason they weren't going to be successful. Don't allow the wrong person to manipulate you into believing that what you desire for your life isn't worth it.

The first thing you have to remember is that you chose or accepted this person into your life. You must take responsibility for your actions. If you are not married to this person, I highly recommend you reevaluate your relationship. Why? Because going after your goals and dreams isn't easy, it's hard as hell. You need to have a person in your life that adds value to your mission. They don't have to be an active partner in the process. You will also need emotional support through encouraging words.

If you are married to your arch nemesis and whenever you discuss success, or personal development, they get blue in the face; I'm not suggesting you disrupt your union. You will need to figure out a way to include them in the vision, based on their needs. If that doesn't work, you have to protect and nurture your vision by keeping them away from it for a season. You will be surprised how quickly opinions change when circumstances are favorable for them.

Remember all challenges are equal and the person you choose to be with will not be the reason you didn't succeed. The advantages in relational problems will arm you for future tough discussions. You learned how to remove yourself from a toxic relationship. You learned how to ignore emotional distractions and focus. As a leader, you learned how to cast a vision that inspired someone who wasn't inspired. You improved upon their courage to step up. You became an influencer.

Race, religion or even the government can be used as excuses. People choose to believe these are the reasons they are not successful. Don't get me wrong, there are always exceptions to the rule. However, a very small percentage of people fall into that category.

I felt I was at a disadvantage when I started my business. At the age of nineteen, I launched my very own home based business; marketing telecommunications, energy, and home services. I had no prior experience in marketing, sales or leadership. At first it was very intimidating. When I was introduced to other professionals in my field, they seemed to have what I refer to as the "it" factor. Their suits were custom tailored, they wore Italian shoes, and they drove luxury cars. They were amazing speakers and trainers – I felt like they were from a different planet! But here I was, a freshman in college and an inner city black kid who spoke ebonics exceptionally well. My previous skill set landed me a job at a nearby campground. I did not have a lot of money to invest in my business. I was ushered into a world that was completely unlike anything I had experienced prior to this moment. I had no experience, no money and no skills. Can you see where this is heading? I have to tell you that for the first few months it was really tough recruiting and getting customers. Why? All my closest friends were financially broke and under the age of twenty-one, with the same disadvantages I had.

Getting customers was not easy. Some of my closest friends and family would not support me. They told me I was being scammed and that my business wasn't going to work. I thought about giving up many times during this period. And now, all of a sudden, those voices were in my head and I began to consider their opinions. Have you ever tried something new and allowed other's opinions to change your perception? This is a very dangerous time in your life. When you allow the opinions of friends and family to persuade your vision, you are giving them the power to keep you in your comfort zone. The problem with staying in your comfort zone is, everything you desire is outside of it.

> *Every day, you have the opportunity to change the direction of your life.*

Early on in my career, I adopted a growth conscious principle: if you buy their opinions, you buy their lifestyle. You had better love their lifestyle before buying their advice. When I first heard this principle, I knew it was true and locked it in my memory. It came from a very successful woman; to whom I owe a great deal. She shared this powerful bite-sized nugget of wisdom and I made the decision to listen to those who were where I wanted to be. I chose the voice that had the lifestyle I wanted for my family. Once the decision was made, all my disadvantages blossomed into advantages; the lack of money forced me to become resourceful. My amateur skill set inspired me to get educated and trained to become a professional network marketer. My poor leadership skills were strengthened through reading a series of self-help books and listening to audios.

My inexperience in business and sales allowed me to learn without limiting belief filters. I may have been naïve, but I felt like I could take on the impossible. Before the decision to persevere was made, I was confronted with a lack of skills I believed were disadvantages. But, when the decision was made to follow the voice of encouragement, all of my disadvantages became advantages. Every day you have the opportunity to change the direction of your life.

I wanted to share this experience, my real life scenario, that required me to learn the Law of Embracement and why it is critically important to get out of your own way. You must let grace step in and carry you to greater heights. Things dramatically improved within one year. By the time I was twenty-two, I had built a million dollar company and generated some serious income.

What disadvantages in your life, could you turn into advantages? My goal throughout this book is to lay out a blueprint that will specifically help you become the best you. No one is exempt from tough times, problems, or failures. Though it may sound cliché, it's not what happens to you, but how you respond that matters most.

Earl Nightingale, one of the greatest thinkers of the twentieth century said, "We become what we think about most." How do you know when you have limiting beliefs? One of the fastest and most effective ways to measure a limiting belief is to look at your bank account. Whether you want to accept this or not, it is the truth. How you value and respect money has a lot to do with your belief system. People with abundant thinking help others, give more freely and allow money to grow. Scarcity thinkers believe they may run out of money and hold it tight, unwilling to help others. They can't see money as energy.

Another litmus test for limiting beliefs is assessing your relationships with friends, family and coworkers. Are they growing and reaching for their dreams? Do they encourage others? Do they enjoy seeing other people do well? If the answer to these questions is yes, then you have some awesome friends. If it's no, then you know where some of the limiting beliefs are coming from. Limiting beliefs are just that: they limit your potential. Human beings have unbelievable potential. An elephant will be an elephant no matter what, but a human being has the potential to become whomever he or she wants to be. And guess what? You too can become whatever you want, and by the end of this book it will be evident.

Here's an example of a limiting belief you may have caught in passing: "Money is the root of all evil." In actuality, it's *the love of money that is the root of evil*, not the money. Have you been raised to believe that money is evil? This could be the reason why there is a lack of it in your life. If that's your belief about money, then you will naturally repel money from your life. All my life, I've known that people with money don't feel this way. Do you know people who have a lot of money that are incredible? Exactly! Money magnifies who you already are inside. If you need growth, it just becomes more apparent when you have money.

This also applies to relationships. If you have been cheated on more than once, you may have the limiting belief that everyone you date cheats. Soon you will start believing that all men or all women are cheaters. This, in fact, is far from the truth. However, your perception has now become a reality. How does this belief limit you? You now enter a relationship with your guard up, and make yourself emotionally unavailable. This behavior isolates the other party emotionally. That person perceives, by your behavior, that you're disinterested. Then they directly, or indirectly, start looking in other places for what's missing in their relationship with you. Most of the time when people cheat, it is not intentional. But their search led them to a situation they handled emotionally. Now you feel like you were right all the time. Why should you even try anymore? It will just happen again. You will continue this pattern from relationship to relationship, year after year.

You must remember that you always have a choice, even when someone close to you has hurt you and emotions are running high. Embrace the experience. There will always be pain when you are giving birth to a new you. By doing so, you give yourself the opportunity to learn the lesson that is required in order to not repeat this class again. It is essential for us to take these important lessons from the past and invest them in the future. Pain allows all of us to discover who we really are. It is during times like these that you learn how you handle challenges. Some people face adversity and thrive, while others hit rock bottom and raise their white flags. You can condition your mind to extract the value from the pain, and learn how to utilize it in the future. It is the Law of Embracement at work.

Remember, fear is not real.

Chapter Two:

Total Ownership

In Life, There Is No Return Policy

This can be a sensitive topic to cover, but this chapter will be life changing, if you can embrace it. There was a time when ownership of assets was extremely well respected. In the twenty-first century, ownership is no longer a glamorous statement. With so many financing and leasing options, it has become the norm not to have ownership anymore. This has trickled down to social responsibilities. No one wants to take full ownership for their mistakes, problems or accidents. Here in the state of Michigan, we have a no-fault law, which means if you get into an accident, it's no one's fault. Say you were driving down the road and a car flew through a stop sign and smashed into you. Under no-fault law, they're not liable for damages. Your insurance company is liable.

When it comes to raising children in the twenty-first century, a lot has changed. I designed an educational curriculum called "Alternative Pathways to Success," which helps children from kindergarten through twelfth grade learn about self-education, leadership, and life skills. I volunteered twice a week, for three hours a day, at a middle school in Detroit. *I needed to bust out of the chains I placed on myself, and thought serving others would be the best way to gain emotional momentum.*

Some of the kids would completely disrespect their teachers, and when they got in trouble, their parents would march into the school and yell at the staff. You could tell these kids weren't raised to be respectful.

Parents today have exempted their children from responsibility. Seeing it so clearly was quite sad. This type of thinking has no real social value. These children will have issues obeying the law, and co-existing with others in the workplace. Worse yet, they will teach this behavior to their own children. That's how it becomes systemic.

Here's a question, and be honest with yourself: Are you constantly complaining and blaming others for your circumstances? Well, if you are unhappy, it's your fault. If you are broke and have been working for years, it's your fault. If you've been trying to lose weight and you haven't, it's your fault. If you're an emotional wreck, it's your fault. It's time for you to step up in your life, take total control and ownership. No one has the power to change your life but you.

I know this may seem harsh, even rude, but I want you to know that the moment you decide to take complete ownership of your life, is the moment everything will begin to change. When you take ownership of your life, you give yourself power to make changes. Now, you understand the psychology of blaming. Blaming others prevents you from accepting your capability to change your own circumstances. As I mentioned in Chapter One, you may not be in control of everything that happens to you, but you can choose to respond differently than you have in the past.

> *The painted canvas of your life will not be perfect, but the colors will represent victories and challenges you have overcome.*

It was not so long ago that I found myself in the valley of self-pity; under the rock of shame. Back in 2010, my ex-girlfriend and I got into a really bad fight. I'm talking verbal conflict, a custodial battle over my daughter, and just blatant disrespect. She knew the easiest way to hurt me was to limit when and how often I could see my daughter. There is nothing I enjoyed more than spending time with my baby girl. She found a million ways to attack me. I'm not saying my actions didn't contribute to her anger. I allowed them to affect me emotionally. It got so bad that I could no longer focus on my life or my work. My passion for helping people waned, and I was broken for the first time in my life. I hit emotional rock bottom.

Whatever your focus is on will expand, and whatever your focus leaves will contract. This situation created a snowball effect in my life. Business slowed down tremendously, so my income dropped and I was unable to pay my bills. This led to stress, anger and frustration. The final phase was depression. I was in this funk for several years. I couldn't seem to break free of this cycle. It seemed like nothing would work and I didn't know what to do.

Friends, family and business partners, tried talking to me but I found myself not wanting to get out of bed. I had very little appetite. I so badly wanted things to change. Deep down inside I knew they would, but I just didn't know when.

So, what was my solution? I had to stop blaming and complaining. I blamed my daughter's mother for my problems. It was her fault that I was suffering and losing sight of who I was. She should help me pay these bills, and the law should force her to help me rebuild my business. There were times that I wanted someone to hurt her because she had hurt me. This thought would flare up during arguments.

I was stuck and didn't know how to get out. Have you ever had a time in your life when you felt like you were face first in dirt, then the dirt suddenly turned to quicksand and every action you took caused you to sink deeper and deeper? That's where I was at, slowly being buried in my own sorrow. It continued to get worse after my vehicle was repossessed. This was such a tough time for me. As a man, I was embarrassed and ashamed of myself.

You may be wondering how I turned it all around. Looking back, I would have to say that it was God's grace and mercy. He helped me recognize that I needed to take full ownership over my life. It was time for me to give my troubles to him. I was ready to take responsibility for my actions.

You can forgive those who hurt you and move forward. I realized that I couldn't keep blaming my daughter's mother. She wasn't thinking about me or the pain her actions caused. I needed to get my life back on track, not only for me, but for my daughter as well. I knew that if I could look up, I could get my butt up. I chose to forgive her – not for her sake, but for mine. I took my focus off blaming and placed it on rebuilding.

You may wonder how I could take ownership for something she did to me. I chose to stop building my business (which led to financial disaster), not because of what she did, but because I was consumed with blaming her and chose to respond that way. It was a choice I made. I learned a very valuable lesson about how feelings can build or destroy a person. Don't think for one moment that I wasn't a little angry or bitter, because I was. No situation you emotionally lived in can be totally wiped away overnight, but the decision to embrace ownership and accountability can set you in a new direction. Today, I am happy to say that my businesses are doing extremely well, my ex and I are civil, and my daughter is doing great. We see each other every other weekend and a lot in the summer.

When you make mistakes or poor choices, you have to remember that we are all human. The painted canvas of your life will not be perfect, but the colors will represent victories and challenges you have overcome. Some days will be filled with blacks and grays. Other days will be painted in bright orange. I do believe that for every dark color, there is a corresponding bright color. You have to know deep down inside that the yellowest sun, the bluest sea, and the whitest clouds are in front of you.

Here are a few tips to help you take control of your life:

#1. Face Your Fears:

What are you afraid of? Moving past fear is essential to taking control of your life, and this is where many people fall short. You have been selling yourself a deed of lies, and now you've become paralyzed by your own conversations in your head. Consider doing the opposite and you will get the opposite result. For example, if you are afraid of rejection, go out and pursue rejection. Experiencing rejection wasn't very popular to me either. I had to overcome my fear of people saying no to my opportunity. First, I became conscious of the story I would tell myself before entering a prospecting opportunity. I silenced the fictitious story. I noticed the audacious voice saying, they wouldn't be interested, or the opportunity isn't for them. Next, I had to remove my emotion from their response. Can you imagine if a waitress got offended when you said "No" to dessert? It would be preposterous. The waitress has zero emotion about your response because you're not saying no to her, you're saying no to your interest in dessert. Please remember, fear is not real.

#2. Doubt is Dangerous:

Don't be so quick to assume you can't accomplish what you set out to do. You have to remember that your past does not equal your future. Before people had success - they didn't. The difference between them and you is, consistent effort on a specific area over an extended period of time. Doubt kills dreams and smothers motivation. Doubt attacks your dreams with a vengeance. Other people's doubt about your dreams can be worse, and you have to protect your mind from opinions. Trust your instincts and follow your purpose.

#3 Dream Big:

Dreaming is nourishment to your mind, body, and soul. Dreams are fertilizer for a happy life. Dreaming connects you with your inner self. It allows you to see a preview of what's to come. Dreams also release endorphins that can positively impact the quality of your health. They give you a chance to escape your present reality. The more acquainted you become with your dreams, the greater the chances are for you to convert them into goals. Subsequently, you will develop more skills, add more value to the market and eventually your goals will become your reality. Always repeat this process with new dreams. What dreams do you have that may have been in storage? If you're going to dream, then be bold and dream courageously.

#4 Be Courageous:

Courage is facing your fears and circumstances head on. It takes a great deal of courage to take control of your life. Many people allow circumstances to dictate their decisions to improve their situations. It doesn't matter if you lack the time, money or education. It's not resources you are in need of, it's the ingenuity to be resourceful. It doesn't matter how long it takes for your life to reach the next level. It's time to become the person you deserve to be. No one is going to save you, but you. Let's get fired up and allow our decisions to dictate our circumstances.

#5 Haters Will Hate:

Once you make a decision to take control of your life, the people closest to you are going to notice. In all honesty, most people you associate with won't understand. They will dispute your new decisions because of their own insecurities. Once you decide to take full ownership of your life, you've also made a decision to head in a different direction. A direction I refer to as "the path least traveled." This is a direction where you make a conscious effort to improve your quality of life.

Most people have become comfortable with mediocrity. By choosing to live better, you become part of a small percentage of people. You now see a brighter future for yourself, but your friends and family may fear losing you as you move to a better position in life. Their hating is nothing more than a last ditch effort to sway you off your new path. I think they know better, but they choose not to do better. Don't be offended, embrace it as a clear sign you are moving in the right direction.

Mastering the struggle requires you to master your emotions.

Chapter 3:

Your Emotional Forecast

Don't Trust Your Emotions - Trust Your Focus

Here in Michigan, we have some of the strangest weather. On Monday, it can be sunny and eighty degrees, and by Tuesday it can be cloudy, rainy and thirty degrees cooler. If you've visited Michigan, then you definitely know this to be true. You may live somewhere that has weather with extreme changes. Just like the weather, our emotions can change hourly. One day we're feeling happy and the next day, one small emotional trigger can make us miserable. Unlike weather, we have the ability to control our emotions. Have you ever had a day when you felt like your emotions were controlling you? It seems like every little thing that could go wrong does, and it drives you nuts.

Let's imagine such a situation. Suppose you leave home tomorrow morning and forget your phone. You'll be late to an important event if you turn around, so you just keep driving. You're flying down the road like a mad person, and after a few miles your tire pops and starts wobbling – it's flat. At this point you're furious, and wondering why all of this is happening to you.

You begin the process of beating yourself up mentally. This

starts with negative body language. When you're upset, and feeling bad, your body responds a certain way. You noticed yourself hunched over, with your shoulders forward and your head down. Next comes the internal beating when you begin to tell yourself how dumb you are, or how this only happens to you. When polluted with negativity, internal conversation is dangerous. You repeat destructive thoughts to yourself throughout the day. Some of you have been handling this kind of situation the same way for decades and wonder why things are not changing for the better in your life. I've been there; I have had things happen in my life that were out of my control. These destructive thoughts would haunt me throughout the day, and I'd go back and forth, wondering what I could have done differently.

Mastering the struggle requires you to master your emotions. You must take full control over your emotional state. This is called managing your state. Often, we place our emotions on autopilot. When you are not in control there is no predictable outcome. Later in the book I'm going to teach you strategies on how to manage your emotional state, which is critical for helping you transition out of your struggle.

My focus here is not to make you emotionless: emotion is essential to your human composition. Destructive feelings or emotions can be anger, fear, doubt, or anxiety. Productive emotions are passion, happiness, certainty, joy, and love. The key to experiencing productive emotions consistently in your life is to make a conscious effort to express them daily. It's simple, but not easy. By expressing productive emotions, you're training yourself to make this your regular attitude. This is no different than changing a diet or workout regimen. It's going to take consistent effort in order to observe satisfactory results. How do you become consistent in new and uncharted territory? You need to gain leverage over yourself. In the

Equipping Phase, I'm going to discuss exactly how to completely overhaul your emotional state. Remember: those who shifted their struggle didn't achieve it by changing their struggle, but by becoming emotionally resilient and mentally fit.

You cannot control the weather, you cannot control your boss, and you cannot control your loved ones. The only thing you have control over is your response to life's challenges. Maturing emotionally begins with *responding* to challenges instead of *reacting* to them. When you react to causes, the effect is usually not good. Someone does something unethical to you in a business deal and you feel outraged and want to get even. Your ex-boyfriend or girlfriend starts dating your best friend, and now you're wondering how long they have been planning to be together. You're thinking to yourself was it during your season with them? How could they do this to you? Your emotions take you on a rampage - keying car doors, breaking windows, and slashing tires. These examples may seem extreme, but people often allow their emotions to hijack their reasoning. When you're emotionally weak, anger resentment and jealousy foster easily.

Your ability to read situations and determine better outcomes is important. When you respond to causes in your life, the effects are positive. You had no control over either of those examples, but you blame yourself.

> *The reason people are unfulfilled is because they know, deep down, they can become so much more.*

You have another choice: you can choose not to engage in thoughts that generate destructive emotions. It's okay to be angry, but it's not healthy to internalize the pain and carry it into your future relationships. Seek wisdom over stupidity.

Emotional Roller Coaster

The summer of 1996 was a very special time for me. A couple of good friends and I were planning to visit Cedar Point to conquer one of the largest roller coasters in the world. We talked about how cool and exciting it would be to ride the Magnum. We heard from friends at school that the Magnum could make a grown man "pee his pants". Hearing a statement like that got us more excited about riding it. Rumor had it, people with weak stomachs vomited all over themselves. When you're eleven years old, this information becomes pretty exciting stuff – I even remember counting down the days. On an early June morning, we left Port Huron traveling to Sandusky, Ohio. When we arrived, we were beyond excited. We headed straight for the Magnum. They said that the wait in line would be about two hours, but we didn't care. Finally, the moment came and we were on the ride.

We strapped ourselves in and braced for a wild ride. Slowly, we pulled off. Soon, there was a slight drop, and we were slung from left to right. Suddenly, we slowed again, and began to climb. We could hear a clicking every few seconds, and I could see the entire park as we got higher. I was both excited and nervous, wondering what I'd gotten myself into. In an instant, everything became a blur. I was screaming at the top of my lungs with fear and excitement. We entered a dark tunnel and a long drop, then a winding pretzel or two. I could hear people screaming, begging to get off. In a little over two minutes, the ride came to an end.

Life will often feel like an emotional rollercoaster. One moment you're having an awesome day and everything appears to be going well. Maybe you got news that your tax refund is twice as large as you expected, and that it showed up in your bank account two days faster than you anticipated. The day after that, the IRS placed a levy on your checking account. The money you needed for your rent, payday loans, and a trip you planned with friends is suddenly gone. This is a perfect example of emotional ups and downs. Learning to manage your feelings is important. Otherwise you become their slave.

Altering your life is going to be a lot like riding the Magnum. The ideal outcome will have you excited and engaged. But once you get started, you will face adverse conditions. Reality sets in and you realize this isn't going be as easy as you thought. The reason most people don't finish the journey they started is because they had the option to quit. Jim Rohn, a great personal development philosopher says, "Changing your life is easy, but it's even easier not to." And I completely agree. Once the roller coaster starts, you don't have the option to get off. You are forced to complete that ride. When you get on the ride, you might start thinking destructive thoughts. In the middle of the ride, your brain, warped by this mindset, might even demand that you jump off to save yourself!

It's now 2015 and here are a few astonishing facts: most people are either dead or dead broke by the age of sixty-five, the average United States household is about $10,000 in debt and four out of ten people hate their careers. The reason people are unfulfilled is because they know, deep down, they can become so much more. Becoming more wasn't easy for me and is not going to be easy for you. It's the same with struggling, but achieving your goals is a worthy endeavor. You will become very happy with the person you become through the process. It won't be the monetary process, or the things associated with it. Instead, it's going to be the moment when you look in the mirror and know you can add value to the world.

As the butterfly flaps its wings to gain momentum for flying,
you will begin to gain traction in the areas
where you once struggled.

Chapter Four:

The Butterfly Process

Get Ready to Spread Your Wings

I am really excited to talk to you about the butterfly process in this chapter. Over the last ten years, I've been on a journey full of ups and downs. I understand my journey isn't the same as yours – no two journeys will be the same.

You have to understand that I was fortunate to have an amazing childhood. I don't have any tragic childhood horror stories that would be gut wrenching. It wasn't until I left home that I began to experience how tough life could be. After having tremendous success for a few years, there's just no way you could have ever prepared me, mentally, for what was going to come right around the next corner. But, before I can describe the butterfly process to you, I need you to promise that you can embrace your own process with honor and dignity. Deal?

Sometimes, all we need is a little perspective; just another way of looking at life's moments. Making the decision to change your life is going to feel small, like a butterfly egg. You won't notice any immediate change. But, over a period of time, because of a simple decision, you will find yourself in a new place. Just like the caterpillar fighting to get out of its chrysalis, you will have to fight to change your life. Embracing its struggle, the caterpillar eats its own shell for nutrients. The very thing that kept it contained is now a source for wellness, nutritional value and growth. The caterpillar will shed many skins over time. As time goes on, you will shed the old you for a new and improved you.

Scientists call this process "instar." This term is a combination of the words "in" and "star." When combined, the meaning of these words is clear: inside, you are a star, but you need to shed the old you. Just as caterpillars are constantly consuming nutrients to prepare for their metamorphosis, you must consume information to prepare for your transformation. In the Law of Equipping, I will explain the information I consumed that guided me out of the jungle of struggle.

Great things are coming to you. You may ask how I know. You might be thinking I don't know you, and haven't met you or spoken with you. That's true, but I can say with certainty that success is your birthright. You were not placed on this earth to be average or ordinary. The fact that you chose to pick up this book and read it tells me that you have great expectations for your life. All I needed to change was some direction and encouragement, and you're no different. In Chapter Three, I mentioned that I started as an entrepreneur at a very young age. When I was growing up, I certainly didn't see myself as a business owner. I actually wanted to be an orthopedic surgeon, so studying biology and Pre-Med in undergrad was a necessity. I was doing exactly what I was schooled to do: graduate from high school, go to college, and pursue a great career. My mother was highly educated. Maybe you can relate or maybe you can't, but I wanted one degree that would pay me well. Once I started shadowing surgeons, I knew it was not the life for me. I began considering law, engineering, and pharmaceuticals, but none of them excited me.

When I was introduced to the concept of residual income and leverage, I was absolutely blown away. It was the most exciting way of earning money that I had ever heard of. Like the caterpillar, I fought and worked extremely hard to achieve success. Within my first eighteen days in business I recouped my initial investment, and in the next twelve days, I generated a profit. I was so excited, and so proud of myself. Honestly, I have to say I got a little cocky. I finally felt that I was good at something, and could be a leader to thousands of independent business owners.

Similar to the caterpillar, I began to shed. I released my young, inexperienced, and boyish skin. I took on the polite, egotistical skin of a cocky young man. But, before long, it was time to shed again: seven months later, at the age of twenty, I found out I was going to be a father.

My first thought was, "Oh no! I'm going to have to tell my mother." I definitely wasn't looking forward to that. But speaking to my mother was a real relief, as she was excited by the idea of a grandchild.

My business was still part-time, so I knew I had to find a more reliable source of income. Looking through the job section of the newspaper, I spotted an ad that read: *Earn $100,000 per year in your first year as a car sales consultant!* I didn't want to be a car salesman, but a car sales consultant sounded prestigious. A gentleman by the name of Purdy answered the phone and invited me to Plymouth, Michigan for a job interview. It was a whirlwind seventy-two hours, from becoming an expectant father to getting a new job.

As you've probably already guessed, I discovered it was a

sales job when I got there. The newspaper ad made me think that a consultant did something different. Purdy did a great job of helping me see the bigger picture, and helping me see the job as an opportunity. He also helped show me the opportunities this job afforded him. I immediately got started. This happened to be my first full-time job with benefits and a 401K plan. As time went on I did well, but I was working twelve-hour shifts, six days a week. I was absolutely miserable with the schedule. Like the caterpillar, I knew this wasn't my life's purpose. And unless I wanted to stay here for the next thirty to forty years of my life, I was going to have to make some major strides in my part-time business. Now, don't get me wrong: I learned a lot, earned a lot, and experienced some awesome moments with clients. But my family was my main focus, and I wanted to get home to them.

There's a part of your brain called the reticular activating system, or RAS for short. This is the part of your brain that filters all incoming information and affects the way you pay attention. When you're outside, your brain is receiving a million inputs from your five senses simultaneously, and there's no way to pay attention to everything at the same time. Your RAS helps you focus on what's important to you at that moment. Say, for example, you decide to purchase a new car, and that you have a make and model in mind. Suddenly, you start to see that exact kind of car everywhere. Your brain has now focused on exactly what you told it to look for.

> ...what I considered to be a standstill was actually God working on me.

I took this approach in business. I found out what the top earners in my industry were reading, and began to read those books. I figured that if it worked for them, it could work for me too. The caterpillar consumes its shell for nutrients; I began to consume new information for mental nutrition.

I thought I was ready to quit my job. In leaving too soon, I made a rookie mistake. This led to a downhill slide for me and my family. I was sure that something would give, and that I'd get a break in business if I just kept going. I continued to consume new information from books and training seminars, and was emotionally tired and frustrated. I didn't know when anything was going to change, and there weren't any clear results to show me that I was on the right track. Looking back, the only thing I relied on was my faith in God. I had a vision, pursued my vision and did my best to leave everything else to God. Sometimes, entrepreneurs or leaders can be control freaks, and I'm no different. I was pretty horrible at relying on our creator, but there was something I didn't understand: what I considered to be a standstill was actually God working on me. I couldn't see that I had now entered the cocoon phase.

In this phase, nothing seems to be happening in the physical realm, but in the spiritual realm, you are being strengthened by your struggles. You cannot go and achieve your greater purpose with your current skill set. You're going to have to go through a rigorous refining process, and it will not be pleasant. You can either choose to grow, or God will choose for you. When it's time for the cocoon to hatch and the butterfly to be released, you will know that you've been prepped for flight. As the butterfly flaps its wings to gain momentum for flying, you will begin to gain traction in the areas you once struggled in. But, before flight, you have to remember that your wings are new. They have to be expanded and strengthened before they can elevate you. In other words, small breakthroughs will compound before the miraculous happens and takes you to new heights.

Attracting the woman or man of your dreams, or landing an interview that you've worked long and hard for are examples of small breakthroughs. When you receive your tax refund, you still have a responsibility to treat the money right. Learn to invest instead of spend. Every year, around January, people get this itch that a huge financial windfall is coming for them because of taxes. Between December and February, your TV is going to be loaded with tax commercials, trying to help you find ways to spend your tax refund. Maybe you've noticed that this is a pattern people fall into each and every year. There's always a list of things they want, filled with stuff like a new car, a vacation, or new furniture for the house.

If you truly desire to change your struggle, you're going to have to be disciplined and make some different decisions. As I mentioned before, try doing the opposite to receive the opposite. That's a very simple philosophy to live by when you're focused on changing your life. New furniture is not essential to helping you solve your problems. You should consider taking your refund money and identifying ways to make it grow. Buy some undervalued items on Craigslist and resell them. Take an online trading course, and you will learn a skillset that can help you grow your money.

You're entering a new relationship, and everything is going well. This person seems to have all the qualities you've been looking for. You've given yourself time and space to heal from your last relationship, and you know that you want to move forward. This still doesn't mean you're ready to soar. Theodore Roosevelt would say that this represents a second chance to begin more intelligently. You have a chance to ask the right questions during the interview process, check their moral compass, and see what vision they have for their life in the next five years. As we all know, everything that glitters is not gold.

After five long years on the job, you've worked your behind

off for this very moment. The job you've been seeking to take your career to the next level and enabled you to live a better quality of life, has just now presented itself to you. The interview was stellar and they absolutely adored you, but it doesn't mean that you're ready to soar. If you don't get the job, it doesn't mean they don't value you or that you weren't good enough. It may mean that there's a bigger purpose out there for you and your current job is grooming and refining you for that moment. What moment? The moment when you defy all odds, when you begin to flap your wings and elevation takes place and you can now soar over adversity, fear and problems. You have now embraced your struggle and it's time to take things to the next level.

Law 2: Engagement

You must be a part of your own rescue:
The only person responsible for the overall outcome of your life is you. It's your responsibility to make the necessary corrections and changes to live a great life. Your family, friends, and co-workers do not determine your quality of life; only you have that power.

Human nature is funny: we tend to want what we can't have, and we're motivated by the fear of what we stand to lose, instead of what we hope to gain.

Chapter 5:

Push and Pull Philosophy

The Emotional Tug of War

When it comes to struggling, many of us know it best. There's no question that in the twenty-first century, more and more people are struggling at a greater and higher level. The push and pull philosophy is pretty simple: if you like it, you'll pull it close to you, and if you don't like it, you'll push it away. Have you ever been in a relationship where you tried to push a person away? The more you pushed them away, the more they wanted to get close to you. On the flip side, maybe you tried pulling someone close to you. Because you kept pulling, and it was obvious that they didn't want to be pulled, they moved away in a hurry. This is the effect of the push and pull philosophy. You have probably experienced push and pull with a great sales professional. Or maybe it occurred when you were purchasing a big ticket item, even if it was something small, this philosophy was used to convince you to buy.

In my early twenties, I sold cars for Victory Honda in Michigan. Victory was one of the largest and most successful dealership groups in the nation. I knew I had a customer on the hook when I asked them if they wanted to go home and think about if they were ready to purchase the car, and they would refuse. Human nature is funny: we tend to want what we can't have, and we're motivated by the fear of what we stand to lose instead of what we hope to gain. Every day, customers would enter the dealership acting as if they were on a covert mission to purchase a new vehicle. Customers really want a new vehicle, but because of fear, they put up this defense mechanism to push the sales consultant away. You might ask, why would someone walk into a dealership and pretend they don't want to buy a new car, knowing that's why they are there? It didn't make a lot of sense to the sales force. There are so many positive benefits for a customer purchasing a new vehicle. There is a chance to reduce repair costs, improve the maintenance timeline, and just feel better emotionally. I'm sure that you've personally experienced the feeling of owning a new car. It doesn't matter if the car is five years old or brand new. It always feels good to get a new ride.

> *I've learned over the years that when facing struggles in your life you have to choose fear or faith.*

I used the car buying experience as an example, but you can relate this philosophy to almost any area of your life. Push and Pull philosophy if used incorrectly will prevent you from achieving maximum physical health, mental health, and healthy relationships. Why do people put themselves through this? It's very simple; we are either seeking pleasure or avoiding perceived pain. Most people associate the word struggle with pain, and therefore avoid it at any cost.

We all struggle with decision making, communicating with others, or the threat of being taken advantage of. I remember one guy in particular, John, who entered the dealership on a Monday afternoon. He was dressed very casually – nothing alarming – but he had a demeanor that said, "Please do not talk to me." I walked over to introduce myself, and his first words to me were, "I'm not buying a car today." I replied by saying, "That's okay, how can I help you anyway?" As you can see, already he was pushing me away. This man began to explain that his current vehicle was on its last leg as it had over one hundred thousand miles on it, I agreed. He was at the dealership because his car was due for a new oil change, and the wheels were showing a lot of wear and tear.

In a nonchalant tone, I said, "It sounds like a new car is needed to me." John looked over at me with a blank stare, and said, "I'm not buying!" The whole time he'd had his eye on this beautiful white Honda Ridge Line truck that was in the middle of the show room. It was top of the line and fully loaded. I'm talking chrome rims, tinted windows, heated leather seats, and premium sound. John could not take his eyes off this vehicle, and no matter what he said, I knew he was here to buy. I asked if it was okay to do a quick demonstration of the vehicle to help him understand its features and benefits. I took him around the car, inside the car, and by the time I finished my demonstration he wanted to take the car for a ride.

I grabbed a dealer plate, stuck it on the back of the truck, and said, "Let's take her for a ride." After the test drive, there was no denying it – I knew he wanted this truck badly. I asked, "If I can make the numbers work, do you want to take the truck home today?" He replied, "Because you didn't push me during this process and you allowed me to get to know the product, understand the product, and experience the product, let's see if we can make a deal." John left that day with the truck of his dreams. John was like most people in this situation: most people, when they feel like someone else has superior communication skills, naturally hesitate in their decision making. As you can see from my story, I didn't pull John. What I did in the beginning of our conversation was gently push him away from me, in spite of his hesitancy to buy. Customers typically expect to be oversold, not pushed away.

Whatever struggle you may be dealing with in your life; whether big or small, common or uncommon; it's important not to resist it. It's better to pull it closer to you. Embrace your struggle, because once you embrace it, you give yourself the power to observe and improve your challenge. It doesn't matter if you are having financial challenges, relationship challenges, or health challenges. By openly moving towards your struggles, you will enlist the help of your Creator. When you run from your struggles, you forfeit your power to change your circumstances. We all have failed to address our problems head on. When we look back, we'll admit that we should have made that phone call, asked those tough questions, or simply said I love you to those special people in our lives when we had the chance.

We fail to address our problems face to face because we want to avoid what I call "virtual pain." Unlike dogs or cats, humans have a way to associate specific actions with mental pain. It boils down to fear of rejection or being hurt. Fear and faith cannot occupy the same space in your mind at the same time. I've learned over the years that when facing struggles in your life you have to choose fear or faith. In Chapter 15, I'm going to provide a strategy to strengthen your faith. How do you know which one you chose? When you have chosen fear, you will push your problem away; when you choose faith, you'll take ownership, and pull your problem toward you. Later in this book, I will explain the advantages of owning your struggle versus renting your struggle.

The only way to avoid making mistakes would be to do absolutely nothing.

Chapter 6:

Make Mistakes

Mistakes Bring Clarity

There's no question that we've all made mistakes in our lives. There isn't a lot I can guarantee, except that you will make more mistakes. Mistakes are a quintessential part of life, and it's our responsibility to gain insight from them for preemptive purposes. Making mistakes is a necessity – the problem comes when you repeat the same mistakes continuously. In order for your quality of life to improve, you are going to have to take full responsibility for all actions and consequences. Otherwise, your life will be like driving on the highway on a foggy day, fearful and cautious of what hazards lie ahead. It will be as if you are driving while looking in the rearview mirror the whole time. Mistakes aren't designed to paralyze you; they're crafted to educate, encourage and move you in the correct direction. I want you to know up front that you are not your mistakes. Don't allow your mistakes to define you. Don't allow anyone else to define you either, only you can define you. A mistake is nothing more than an error in judgment, and the cool thing is that you have the ability to fix it. The only way not to make mistakes would be to do absolutely nothing. You would have to live a life of solitude and take very minimal actions. Can you imagine how boring that would be? In my professional opinion, it would be a total waste of living. Without mistakes, there is so much innovation humanity would have squandered. Before I wrote this book, I understood the perplexities readers have about the fear of making mistakes. To get engaged in your struggle, you're going to have to make additional mistakes.

Let's take a quick look at some very significant leaders who made huge mistakes. In order to get the light bulb correct, Thomas Edison had to make 9,999 mistakes. So that you could fly in an airplane today, the Wright brothers had to make some huge design and engineering mistakes.

When Los Angeles Laker Kobe Bryant made a mistake in Colorado, it cost him millions of dollars in endorsements, and almost cost him his marriage and family. Through all the scrutiny and agony, Kobe learned from his mistakes and returned to the court stronger, faster, and more competitive. This is all because he learned from his mistakes; because he turned his mistakes into emotional fuel to dominate his craft.

Now, let's talk about you. Whatever you may be struggling with can shift in a moment. Understand; you're going to have to get comfortable with the idea of being uncomfortable. Mistakes are only a representation of your steps in a new direction. If you don't change, everything will remain the same. But if you choose to change, you will know you have grown because you're comfortable with what used to make you uncom-fortable. Our brain is wired so that it receives information better and more permanently when an experience is attached to it. Naturally, when you don't make mistakes, you don't learn.

Why are you so afraid of making a mistake? Is it because you are worried about making the wrong decision? Are you concerned what your peers may think if you quit your job and start a business you have always dreamed about? I am not suggesting that you quit your job prematurely. It could be that, when you were a child, you got schooled on security as opposed to calculated risk and opportunity. Maybe you've had bad experiences, and these experiences scared the hell out of you. Fear encourages you to do what is easiest. Doing what's easiest doesn't strengthen you and if you're not being strengthened you are not growing. When you fear confronting the decision in front of you, you can count on having to relive that experience.

I think the biggest reason we fail to make even more audacious mistakes is due to the educational system. We were taught to go to school, get good grades and successfully pass the test. But what happened when you didn't do so well on a test? You were reprimanded or verbally scolded for your less than perfect performance. Naturally, this made you feel reluctant to make mistakes. What's funny is that the system starts at age five and goes until age twenty-one. For sixteen years, it has been ingrained in our subconscious mind that mistakes are unacceptable. This is why a majority of people spend the rest of their lives avoiding dream exploration. We have an educational system that rewards perfection, which is absolutely ridiculous because no one is perfect. If you haven't heard, allow me to be the first to tell you that this system is obsolete. This is why, in order to master any craft, art, or profession, you have to start as an amateur. During the amateur stage, making mistakes is essential in the development of skills and knowledge necessary for success in a specified area.

We were always taught that knowledge is power, but I'm here to tell you that knowledge is only potential power. Without action, you cannot have a reaction. You have to remember that mistakes are necessary for success. I live by the philosophy that new levels require new skills. Children are some of the greatest leaders and educators in our society. My son is two and a half years old, and he is in his last phase of potty training. As a parent, you already know that we've had some accidents in this process. There will be successes and there will be failures. Typically, failures require clean underwear or cleaning a mess off the floor. When our children make mistakes, whether with potty training or learning their ABCs, we encourage them to keep trying.

It would be kind of silly if we told them to stop trying or to just give up when they make mistakes. By nature, we are natural encouragers, and when our children are going through challenges we encourage them to persevere through it. Don't you think you should do the same thing for yourself? Why don't you? Now that you're an adult, are you too old to encourage yourself or other adults? Again, I just wanted to give you some additional perspective on how to look at mistakes. Please remember that you need mistakes in your life to witness progress.

Change is inevitable, but progress is not. No pushing past our instincts or intuition. I think spirituality is a key element in our lives. I'm personally a believer in God; however, I respect all spiritualties. I feel it's just important to find something that is bigger than you to believe in. I want you to think about some past experiences you recently went through. Do you remember telling yourself, "Something told me?" We all have a built-in directional system. It is truly a gift from our Creator. This internal system guides us on a daily basis to keep us on track. Whether you know it or not, your life has a great purpose. And your personal GPS is designed to keep you on the right path.

Just like when we're driving, we can sometimes get off route. When we do, our GPS system recalculates us. Typically, the recalculation takes us a little bit longer to get back on our original route. And most GPS systems have a voice. I don't have a name for mine but you may. By now, you have probably noticed that you also have a voice that guides your life. The challenge is, this voice is very quiet and subtle. It's not pushy or demanding. I call this your Angel voice, we all have it and need to be able to listen to it.

Every time you make a decision, you will always hear this voice speaking. Most often we push past the voice because logically it doesn't make sense at the moment. But then you find yourself wishing you had followed that first thought, that first mind, or that first instinct. The key to minimizing your mistakes is developing the discipline necessary to follow and trust this voice consistently. This task is not easy. But if success was easy, everyone would achieve it, right? So, your goal over the coming weeks is to listen to this voice. It may happen when you're driving, brushing your teeth, or sitting at work. The voice could tell you to make a call, to turn left, or that the fast food you're eating isn't good for you. Throughout the day, you make a ton of decisions. To minimize error, you're going to have to listen to your Angel voice. It is here to guide and protect you.

It's not a poor decision that leads to a poor life; it's a series of poor decisions that leads to a poor life.

Chapter 7:

Better Decisions

Better Decision Making Leads to an Extraordinary Life

Your decisions are nothing more than the solutions from your thoughts. As I mentioned before, your thinking is a series of questions and answers in your head. Your current struggle is a reflection of past decisions. As bad as it may sound for some, you are actually where you decided to be. There's a line in *Forrest Gump* that reminds me of how most people live their lives. It's when Tom Hanks says, "My mama always said, life is like a box of chocolates – you never know what you're going to get." I can bet that ninety-five percent of the audience that heard that quote agreed, and five percent of the audience disagreed. Ninety-five percent of the population believes that your circumstances determine your life, while the other five percent believes that your decisions determine your lifestyle. The primary difference between the two groups is that one group takes control over their life, while the other group gives their control away.

If this is your first time reading a book involving personal development, this may be a breakthrough concept for you. Most people never evaluate the decisions they make and the consequences produced from their decisions. Let's take eating ice cream as an example. It's fine to have a scoop of ice cream, but imagine you had ice cream four or five times a week for thirty-six months. Then your lack of discipline would create a problem. You would probably gain somewhere between five and fifteen pounds, have clogged arteries, and would probably be approaching diabetes. Your decision making process is very similar to this: small errors in judgment compounded over a long period of time lead to major problems. You and I are human, and we are going to make poor decisions. In the next section, I'm going to discuss how to become better at making decisions. It's not a poor decision that leads to a poor life; it's a series of poor decisions that will lead to a poor life. Do you know what the definition of insanity is? I didn't either. It's doing the same thing over and over expecting a different result, according to Albert Einstein. Most people have been insane for years.

When I was five years old, the doctor informed my mother that I had high cholesterol. Keep in mind, I was as skinny as a toothpick, but I would go into the refrigerator every day after school for a slice of cheese. A little bit of cheese isn't bad for you, but that little slice of cheese compounded over a long period of time can kill you. I want you to think about your life for a couple of minutes. Can you think back to the very decision or decisions you have made that placed you in your current situation? Typically, hindsight is 20/20, and your poor decisions can be clearly identified. However, we continue to produce more poor decisions even when we know better. Why is that? It's your decision making formula. Let's break down how people make decisions.

After meeting thousands of people and hearing their stories, I've come up with the following decision making formula: Philosophy + Belief = Decision. Almost every decision you make is based on this formula. You're probably wondering right now how you make this formula work for you instead of against you.

Personal philosophy is different than Greek philosophy. This conversation will not be about Aristotle and his great quotes. Personal philosophy is what you've learned, why you learned it, and how you learned it. Your personal philosophy is what you have come to know at this very moment. There are many things that contribute to your philosophy. Your parents taught you their social and economic philosophies. How you currently interact with people and associate with money comes from your philosophy. Friends have left an impression on your philosophy. The educational system and media outlets like social media, television and radio all affected what you know today.

The most effective way to change your philosophy is to acquire new information. The information can come from multiple sources. You now have the choice to read books, associate with new friends, and reduce entertainment. When you begin to invest your time in reading or listening to books designed to radically improve your health, wealth, and spiritual being, improvement is inevitable. Belief is certainty about something. Some people believe that success comes from luck. You may believe that you are struggling because of your race or religion. You may believe that your chances to live a great quality of life are lower because of where you live or where you grew up. You are still carrying around those limiting beliefs. I could go on and on: there are thousands of limiting beliefs that we all carry with us.

> *Another important concept to grasp is, there is a difference between a decision and a preference.*

One of my objectives in this book is to help you replace limiting beliefs with empowering beliefs. Personally, I used to believe that I just wasn't good at earning money. I know it sounds elementary, but it drove me crazy. Whatever business I launched made profits, but they always seemed like small profits. I would criticize myself internally about my ability to earn. Naturally, this assessment came from my financial results. It wasn't just in my head – I could see exactly what I was and was not producing. Holding on to these limiting beliefs impacted my ability to increase my profits. I had to change what I believed about myself and my ability to earn money.

The foundation of the change was prayer. I needed God's help. Then I needed to get better at my craft. Instead of buying further into my lack of ability to earn more, I decided to buy into the idea of improving my skillsets. I got better at communicating more effectively by reading books on effective communication. What I learned in those books was reinforced by observing effective leaders in my business, then by me rehearsing what I had learned. I got hooked on leadership expert John C. Maxell's books and YouTube audios. Then I implemented what I learned, reviewed results, and determined if the results were successful. I measured it based on impact and influence. I now call them the Three I's of Leadership: Implement, Impact, and Influence. I saw my skills improve and my ability to earn more became obvious.

The Art of the Struggle was written for you, by someone just like you. I want you to know that I am no different from you. I have seen the good and the bad, and the only difference between us is the new information I decided to internalize; the concept of changing my life. Throughout the book, you will notice specific relationships, how they impacted my life, and what doors led me safely through darkest days of my life. New Philosophy + New Beliefs = Better Decisions, which led to a better life. Remember, the struggle is here to strengthen and refine you, not harm you.

Another important concept to grasp is there is a difference between a decision and a preference. Often, they get confused. This will be the biggest stumbling block you will encounter on the pathway to improving your life. In the past, you may have attempted to use weight loss shakes, seminars, books and audiobooks. You may have experienced momentum for a few months, but it wasn't the lasting change you were seeking. If you truly desire lasting change, then you must understand this concept thoroughly. When you make a decision, you cut off all other possibilities. If you joined a gym, for example, quitting is no longer an option because of your decision to reach your goal.

Preference is a preferred choice or idea. If joining the gym was just a preference, then quitting could be an option once things got tough. Decisions are nothing more than a strong commitment. One of my mentors described commitment as, "Doing what you said you were going to do long after the emotion you said it with has passed." The gym idea may be a little cliché, but it serves as the best illustration. At the beginning of every year, people set New Year's resolutions to have more money, have better relationships and to lose weight. By February, ninety-five percent of people who set a New Year's resolution quit, because it wasn't a decision.

On the other hand, do you remember a time when you said enough was enough; that something or other would never happen again, and it didn't? That was a decision. In order to keep your decision, you have to get enough leverage on yourself. Leverage is having enough reasons to follow through on your goals. If you give yourself enough reasons to lose weight, you will. If you give yourself enough reasons to earn more money, you will. And guess what? If you give yourself enough reasons to get out of your struggle, you will! The beautiful part about your life is that you have the choice to change everything right now.

I recently got married to the most incredible woman ever. I truly believe the divorce rate is so high because couples made a preference to get married, but not a decision. If you talk to anyone who has been married twenty, thirty, or fifty years, one attribute they all have in common is that they made a decision to stay married. This decision requires a firm commitment and understanding. You may be a person who really tried to keep your marriage together, but still got divorced. In this case, your partner made a preference and you made the decision to get married. Tony Robbins says, "Once that thing goes from a should to a must, the desired result will take place". I bet right now you could take ten minutes and think about all the things you should do. Why haven't you done them? Because they're *shoulds* and not *musts*. Your whole life is centered on the decisions you make. If you become more efficient in decision making, there is nothing you can't achieve in your life.

Law 3: Equipping

You must have the right tools for the right job:
Becoming more than you already are requires new skills. These skills give you access to new possibilities within yourself. Every leader needs to welcome and add new skills to their human toolbox. These skills include:

<u>Vision</u>: *Seeing beyond your current circumstances.*
<u>Mindset</u>: *Strengthening your mental muscle.*
<u>Standards</u>: *Demanding more of yourself.*
<u>Perspective</u>: *What's true to you will become your view.*

Vision offers you superhero-like powers for transformation.

Chapter Eight:

Vision

You Achieve What You Regularly Envision

Vision is the origin for transformation and achievement. It's the most important tool that you'll need to be equipped with. Your vision will shine light on the right path for you to take. Vision is a clear and vivid expression of what is to come for your life. Maybe through a dream or a daydream, you saw your life differently than it is in its present state. Vision helps us remain authentic to our greater purpose. Pursuing your vision will lead to a fulfilled life. You have to discover what that is for you. Often, life has a way of blinding or distracting us from our vision.

Consider the following questions:

- When you were a child, what did you want to be and why?
- How would your childhood friends have described you?
- What is it that you still enjoy doing today, that you did as a child?
- What would you do even if you could not be compensated for your efforts?

> *Even though you want a quantum leap to happen, be patient. Your time is coming.*

I highly recommend taking some time to reflect over those four questions. Who you truly are will be found in your childhood. Over time, you may have shifted because of circumstances and different life dynamics. If you trust and follow your instincts, they will lead you back to your vision.

Your vision can also be your escape plan from a life of mediocrity. Vision offers you superhero-like powers for transformation. One of my favorite superheroes is Superman. Superman has incredible strength, speed, and the ability to fly. Let's not forget his astonishing x-ray vision. He is almost invincible. But every villain wants to find a superhero's weakness and Superman's Achilles heel was kryptonite. Whenever Superman came near kryptonite, he immediately began to lose his strength. Kryptonite slowly caused Superman to die. And the only way to survive was to get away from it as fast as possible.

I always thought it was cool that the sun restored Superman. In your life, you have kryptonite people or challenges around, and sometimes it feels like it's killing you. The sun is to Superman, what your vision is to you. Your vision will restore you, replenish you, and recharge you. This will define who you really are. I think the biggest difference between a vision and a dream is the degree of clarity. If a dream is a trailer, a vision is the movie. The trailer for an upcoming movie only provides fragments. The movie lays out the plot, catalyst and conclusion. Trust it will be a box office hit because the writer, director, and producer is your Creator.

When I first thought about writing *The Art of the Struggle*, I was deep in the jungle of struggle. Looking at the path ahead, I couldn't foresee a way out. But before 2009, I had my most productive and successful year as an entrepreneur. Everything that could go right was going right. I was earning unbelievable amounts of money, paying debt off, and having the extra cash for whatever I wanted. I was also receiving a ton of recognition from my network marketing company. Achieving the goals I had written about at the beginning of the year was fulfilling. I was dating frequently and traveling. I had the ability to take my daughter shopping and out for fun experiences like the Detroit Zoo, water parks, and ice skating. We could do whatever we chose to do; I had both time and money. And I knew that my vision was coming to fruition. I volunteered with local charities. I helped my mother with many of her financial needs.

Life was incredible, and I was on top of my game. After sacrificing a lot of time and effort to reach this point, I felt I had earned the right to enjoy it. I'm pretty sure you would have felt the same way, but there was one mistake that I made. It was a small mistake, but it led to a miscalculation in judgement, and a decision that caused the total collapse of my business. I made the unconscious decision to stop doing the activities that got me to that place. Success had become a distraction for me. And, like most major shifts in life, it is not noticed until it's too late. Devastating choices start out as small as a snowflake falling from the sky. As more fall over time, they turn into a pile of snow. The snowflakes continue to fall, and that pile grows. Just one small noise can release thousands of pounds of snowflakes. Before I could make adjustments, the largest avalanche I had ever seen was heading in my direction.

There was nothing I could do at that point. When business slowed down, more money was going out than coming in. That, is a recipe for financial disaster. I was arrogant enough to believe that I had the power to correct it immediately – I thought I was that good – but my absence of focus for nine months could not be fixed in three weeks. To preserve the image I had fashioned, I borrowed money from family with payback timeframes that were unrealistic. Again, I thought I was that good. At the age of twenty-four, I had generated more than $80,000 in six months. I didn't think it would take much to get back into my old momentum. I didn't have a dime saved or an asset to sell. Financially, mentally, and emotionally I was broke and unable to financially support my daughter. Bills were piling up, and I was barely holding on to my Cadillac CTS.

As time went on, I found myself mentally checking out. I was so caught up with my problems that I was barely present with my family and friends for discussions. The time spent with my daughter wasn't nearly as enjoyable as it used to be. I was hurting inside, and didn't know what to do. I had faced challenges before and overcome them, but this one was unlike anything I'd experienced. I felt like my face was in the mud and a 600 pound elephant was sitting on me. There was absolutely nothing I could do. I went from being the victor to being the victim. I was blaming, complaining, and justifying, telling myself this was unfair. I would lie in bed asking God to take the pain away. I would go through the day with an ache in my stomach. My stress levels were so high that the back of my neck started to hurt. I tried to find jobs, but they wouldn't hire a college dropout turned entrepreneur.

I needed to earn money immediately. My mother was amazing through this process. I am so grateful that she never wavered in her support. But while my face was submerged in the mud, I couldn't hear or see what she was trying to do for me. She only wanted the best for her son, but my hurt ego edged out her voice of reason. Even though my emotions were up, down, and all over the place, I never lost sight of my vision. Not for one moment did I believe this was my final destination.

I discovered how to strengthen my connection with God. I made it a daily routine in the shower to pray and give God praise. I'm not sure what it was about the water, but the feeling of it would bring a sense of clarity and warmth. This ritual allowed my vision to be preserved, and as time went on it allowed my vision to expand. In the shower, I was able to see how bright my future was. On some very bad days, I would take multiple showers to relieve the pain. This activity allowed me to shed the emotional pain enough to see what was lying ahead. I kept convincing myself that I was here to do great things. I believed I would be wealthy, and that I would serve God's kingdom with the highest honor. Remember, the shoes you fell into the valley with, will not be the shoes you're wearing when you climb out. Even though you want a quantum leap to happen, be patient. Your time is coming. My vision gave me perspective, and that perspective gave me hope. When I was nineteen I asked God to bless me with substantial wealth. I had forgotten what I had asked God for. Because it was so huge, the refining process had to be rigorous and hectic.

Whenever you are giving birth to a new you, there will be labor pains. My vision protected me from believing what my eyes were seeing. Circumstances can manipulate you into believing that your struggle is permanent. Without vision, I would have perished, given up, there's no question about it. You have to take time nourish your vision. Consistently investing time in your vision is paramount. I believe that everyone is given an amazing vision for their life. The challenge is overcoming your doubt about achieving this vision. The more I envisioned, the more I believed it was possible to triumph.

I think it's important for you to visit your future often. Rewind twenty years ago in your mind. The decisions you made then, until now, produced the life that you are currently living. Your finances, your health, and your relationships were produced from past choices. If you are not living the life you envisioned a few years back, then it is important to spend more time in the future, with a new and enhanced you. This exercise will help you to make better decisions in the present. Make decisions that the future you will be happy with. This frame of thinking will help. You will be encouraged to only make conscious decisions that are congruent with your vision. If your vision is to attend college three years from now, there are a series of key decisions that are required to fulfill your vision. If you don't fulfill those requirements, there's no way you can fulfill your vision. So, the future "you" relies on the present you to make the right decisions. I hope this isn't confusing. Your vision and decisions must be congruent in order for your dreams to become a reality.

How Do You Develop a Compelling Vision?

You must begin with the outcome in mind. In the end, how do you want to be remembered? What did you achieve? Do you want be remembered for your contribution to society, science, or the economy? Do you want to be remembered for volunteering and helping those in need? Do you want be remembered for creating a cure for an illness? What do you find yourself continuously dreaming about? These are all questions you must ask yourself daily. Make a list of questions to ask yourself daily, and ask them until you have the answers. Quality questions will lead to quality answers. Either your answers provide emotions that produce motivation, or they provide emotions that produce discouragement.

I think it's easier than ever before to create a vision for your life. With the invention of the internet, we are able to access travel locations around the world and information at lightning speed. No matter what your interest may be in, you can find the necessary resources right now. Vision boards are also a great resource. To make a vision board, take pictures from articles that are related to your dreams and goals, and place them on a bulletin board. Place it somewhere that you look frequently to keep your vision at the front of your thoughts. You need to solidify your vision in your subconscious. This will require that you see it, believe it and cherish it!

*In order to respond, you must acquire the ability to step back
and gather yourself before engaging.*

Chapter 9:

Mindset

If You Set Your Mind in the Right Direction - You Will Arrive at Your Dream Destination

In order to change your current struggle, you're going to have to set your mind in a new direction. Your quality of life is going to be based on the quality of your thinking. It's important to know that your best thinking has gotten you right where you are. Just as someone helped me shift my thinking, I want to help you strengthen your mental muscle. I will be your mental trainer, and my responsibility is to help you get into top mental shape. Like your body, when the mind is weak, it is more susceptible to illness. These illnesses are worry, doubt, fear, poor perspective, neglect and negative self-talk. They are the equivalent of cancer in the body. They begin small and undetected, but over time they take root and begin to destroy your life.

Your mind is like a lump of clay, and with the proper guidance and technique you can sculpt it into a masterpiece. Because of all the challenges you've experienced so far, and more importantly, the challenges you'll face moving forward, mindset is so important. It is imperative for you to have a sound mind and attitude. If you do, you will make sound decisions that will produce a sound life.

At this point, you may be wondering what I did to shift my mindset. I'm going to cover five key traits that will help you develop an effective mindset. It's not money that's going to help you get through life's challenges, but a great mindset. I want to help you avoid the psychological traps that have restricted many from becoming great.

#1 Physical Health:

I am not an expert on health and wellness, but I do understand the importance of proper health. There is no wealth without your health. When you make the decision to change your life, it's going to require energy, vitality and mental awareness. All these traits are produced through a good diet and exercise. Otherwise, your mind will be leading the charge and your body will still be in bed. Start small and gradually work your way to excellence with your health.

#2 Hope:

This happens to be one of the strongest words in any language. It may seem very dark in your life, or things are just not in your favor. Having hope gives you the ability to expect great things to come in your life. When Louis Zamperini was captured as a POW in World War II, he was faced with terrible circumstances. Louis and his officers were on a raft in the middle of the Atlantic for more than forty days without proper supplies. He thought that he was going to die at sea, but they were captured by the Japanese. He was beaten on a daily basis, barely fed, and severely tortured for years. But Louis retained hope throughout this nightmare. Hope gave him the strength to smile during one of the most traumatic times in his life. He felt

God had kept him alive for a reason. Because of his hope, he was the only one who returned back to his family mentally stronger and sharper than before he left. You have to incorporate hope into your daily diet of inspiration.

#3 Self-Starter:

To be a self-starter means that you can't, you won't rely on other people, environments or favorable conditions to motivate you. There isn't going to be a perfect time or season to change your life. If you want to end your current struggle, it's going to be up to you. I know it would be easier to have someone take you by the hand, help and educate you, but even a mentor can't do the work for you. This is the time that you need to step up and take total control. This is going to require massive action on your part.

#4 Self-Discipline:

We live in a microwave society. We're used to having everything instantaneously. This has conditioned us to have a lack of self-control. One of the most important attributes of success (we define success as achieving a worthy goal) is delayed gratification. Your ability to adjust your thinking patterns from immediate expectation to long term gratification is essential. We tend to associate discipline with pain. That's because we can't see an immediate reward for our efforts. There is no such thing as overnight success beyond the lottery. And even lottery winners, in most cases, get their winnings over a long period of time. Improving your life is going to take focused and consistent effort without seeing immediate rewards. Are you game?

#5 Manage Emotions:

This is probably the toughest one. When you are angry or upset, it's always easiest to express how you feel without restraint. The real test becomes how to channel your heightened emotions into productive results. People with successful mindsets gain the ability to control their emotions. After I learned this skill, I was able to set myself free emotionally. That skill set happens to be my ability to respond instead of reacting. I learned from Jack Canfield, author of *Chicken Soup for the Soul*. He said, "Responding is positive and reacting is negative." In order to respond, you must acquire the ability to step back and gather yourself before engaging. You will have the secret to happiness. When people are being nasty, rude, or blatantly disrespectful, it's often an internal problem they are dealing with. You must no longer allow their issues to become yours. I want you to know that no matter how great or terrible your life may seem; you still have the ability to adopt and grow these traits.

There is a distinct difference between a fixed mindset and a growth mindset. Most often, a fixed mindset no longer feels the need to learn and become better. One with a growth mindset remains a consummate learner. Which one are you? You are not chained to your current capabilities. Your brain is very malleable. Just like metal or clay, it can be transformed. Many of the greatest achievers were once looked on as failures; people like Charles Darwin, Thomas Edison, Oprah Winfrey, Albert Einstein, and Wolfgang Amadeus Mozart. I saw a TEDx talk on YouTube, given by Eduardo Briceño. He gave an extraordinary message about fixed mindset versus growth mindset.

Briceño stated, "Under a neuro brain scan of a person with

a fixed mindset the brain becomes most active when receiving input about how they performed, such as a grade or score. A growth mindset brain became most active when receiving input about how they can do better." Science has proven that if you take on the belief of a growth mindset, you can learn and master any area of your life. Your most challenging obstacle will be your mind. Any time we enter uncharted territory, our mind naturally goes into defense mode, protecting us and trying to make us believe that what we are attempting is dangerous. This is the reason trying new things can seem uncomfortable. When the voice of your fixed mindset says, "You don't have what it takes," you should add, "yet." It's important to follow up with the process of improvement and not the results. It really is all in your mind.

You should decide to love freely, eat healthier, start a business, spend more time with family, contribute to your community, wake up earlier, and be on time to work.

Chapter 10:

A New Era of Standards

As Your Standards Improve - Your Overall Performance Improves

In the twenty-first century, competition among individuals in a variety of areas has become fierce. One of the most important tools in your transformational toolbox is standards. The first area of your life that has to improve is what you define acceptable or unacceptable. I didn't realize I had to elevate my standards until I got around people who had standards higher than my own. I'm not talking about dating standards or the car you should drive to impress people. I mean internal standards, what you should expect and demand from yourself. Your life at present is a mirror image of your current standards. Your standards are reflected in your relationships, career, and finances. Pretty much your entire lifestyle is founded by standards. Your standards have been subconsciously ingrained in your life by your current philosophy. Your entire life has been governed by your standards. I don't believe you're learning anything new, but I want to remind you about a few key concepts that will help you raise your standards.

Every year, at the end of December and the beginning of January, people are setting New Year's resolutions. There's something magical about the calendar that allows you to feel like you have a chance each year to start over, improve, and resolve challenges from the previous year. Statistics show that ninety percent of people with a New Year's resolution quit by the fifteenth of January.

This process provides a new perspective about life and destiny. Each year, everyone wants a better sense of control over their life, and making New Year's resolutions provides them with the possibility. The real concern is why so many people are unable to follow through with their resolutions. Have ever you set a New Year's resolution and didn't achieve it? I was one of the statistics, one of those who didn't accomplish my resolution. I remember John Maxwell saying that he didn't set resolutions, but created a plan to grow into his goals. I decided to follow suit.

The word resolution means to resolve or find a solution again. Let's look at the three main problems people are trying to solve every year: 1) earn more/save money, 2) better diet/lose weight, and 3) better career. With all of the information available to us, why aren't people finding success in solving their problems?

You may think this is overly simplistic, but I know it to be true. Tony Robbins says, "It's a should, not a must." Human beings always get their musts. Everything you have in your life right now is based on your must haves. You may say, "Reggie, circumstances and problems are the reason I live the way I do. What are some of the things I should do?" You should decide to love freely, eat healthier, start a business, spend more time with family, contribute to your community, wake up earlier, and be on time to work. These are all things that you should do, but what you have to do now is gain the assurance to make them musts. The way you make them musts is by finding reasons to attach them to yourself.

Most people are always looking for the "how to" factor. Before you know how you are going to do something, you need to establish a strong enough purpose. Willpower is required to push yourself, and willpower never lasts. When you are drawn to your purpose, you will discover unlimited resources within you to achieve it. As I mentioned earlier, it wasn't until I digested this information that I could truly learn how to elevate my standards. I have a great friend who has a successful marriage, and he and his spouse set very high standards. Some of their fundamental standards are:

✓ to never go to bed upset,
✓ to always have a date night,
✓ and to honor one another daily.

These standards have allowed them to remain married for thirty-five years. These standards are a must in their relationship. You may not always achieve your goals, but you can always meet your standards. Your standards will require discipline, but they will become your habits over time.

Self-Identity

Often, we work really hard to consistently maintain our identity. You may think you're talented, savvy, persuasive, and incredibly good looking. Some of you believe that you're an average thinker, okay looking, not very well dressed, terrible at dancing, and socially awkward. Then there are some, who identify themselves as the absolute worst possible person on planet earth.

The reason personal innovation and achievement become so very challenging is that we are as stubborn as mules. Being what my grandmother called "thick headed," most people don't even know who they really are. For decades, people wander through life wondering who they are and what they are here for. Your friends, family, or coworkers may have told you how they view you, and maybe you embraced their picture of you. Everything you do has to remain congruent with this picture you have of yourself. So here's the challenge: If you're going to elevate your standards, you are going to have to let go of how you currently identify yourself and begin a new identity.

Say for example, that you always wanted to become a teacher. Maybe your family helped you impose a belief on yourself that becoming a teacher is not a worthy cause. Following this self-imposed belief, you decided to become a doctor. The fact remains that you would have been a lot happier if had you become a teacher.

What qualities do you admire about accomplished people? Write them down. You just described your new identity and now it's time to take action to become what you designed.

Consistency

Starting and stopping continuously is the definition of inconsistency. This thinking pattern has beleaguered people for centuries, and has prevented them from changing their lives. When you are approaching a new habit, your biggest obstacle will be finding consistency until the habit becomes a new behavior. Anything you've ever done well; you were consistent with. When you're emotionally stimulated, it's often easy for you to continue that activity.

I used to be an avid basketball player. I would spend an entire summer day dribbling a basketball, shooting hundreds of jump shots, and playing pickup games. No matter how hot it was, I could spend the entire day playing basketball. My friends would come over and I'd host tournaments in front of my house from ten a.m. to ten p.m., three or four days a week. This would continue for the entire summer. By the time school started and basketball season came around, all the work in front of the house paid off.

Achievement requires consistency. If you went on a diet and lost weight, it was because you were consistent. If your child does a great job communicating at a young age, it's because you were consistent in communicating with them. To have an amazing relationship with your husband or wife requires consistency. But imagine being in a marriage where some days you show affection and some days you don't. Imagine that on some days you tell them you love them, while on other days you don't. There is no way to have a great relationship without consistency. In relationships, having the feeling of certainty is important. You want to feel like your spouse cares about you. When someone tells you every day that they love you, they do. When someone demonstrates their love for you, it helps you feel certain about how they feel.

In order to turn your circumstances around, it's going to require your full focus and consistent effort. You can't work toward becoming a better person a few times per week. You have to make a firm commitment to apply some of these strategies daily. Work on your needs with the same consistency you bring to brushing your teeth or washing up.

The best way to create a new habit is to automate the process. Use your digital device and set timers to remind you throughout the day to eat correctly, read, or listen to an audiobook. With the distractions of life, you're going to have to use your recreational time. This is the time that you would normally waste on mindless relaxation. This time is normally wasted in front of the TV, on the phone, or at a lounge. This is about ten to fifteen hours a week. You can at least take fifty percent of that and invest in you. Trust me, it is time well spent.

*Whether you want to be a lawyer or doctor, it doesn't matter –
you need to get perspective and information from
those who've achieved in this area.*

Chapter 11:

Purposeful Perspective

Seek Understanding that Provides Value to You

The way you perceive the world, directly affects the way you live your life. The information that you've collected, through your experiences and foundational philosophies, will yield a perspective for your life's outcome. Your perception defines what is true to you. But if you don't continue to grow, you will always have a limited view of yourself and the world that you live in.

People who see the goodness in the world naturally live a life of happiness. Those who see the negatives in the world usually live a negative life. Both people believe they're right, and can thoroughly support their views. Sometimes, you just need a purposeful perspective to give you a refreshing look on how you perceive a situation. We decide, and then give meaning to our problems. You can ask why is God condemning you or you can thank God for making you stronger and wiser. I choose to see the greater purpose in all problems, and you can too. That's why I refer to it as purposeful perspective.

It's not what happens to you that really matters; it's how you view and respond to it that determines the real outcome. I'm going to walk you through several different scenarios to show you the difference between a non-purposeful perspective and a purposeful perspective. I think you'll be able to see which one could begin to add value to your life. Remember, purpose gives us energy, excitement and ambition. All these attributes help you get closer to achieving your goal.

When I'm driving, I often reflect on past responses and reactions to different events in my life. There's something about being in the car that allows me to have transparency of thought. Whether it's on the open road or I'm backed up in traffic, somehow, I find a way to mentally escape. I recommend discovering a place where you can mentally escape. If you haven't already, make it a consistent routine in your life to find time to think for yourself. You want somewhere that won't be influenced by any media or peers, where it's just you and your maker.

Failure to Succeed

Too often, the struggle is real: life has a way of challenging you constantly. You may feel the struggle to provide adequately for your family, to be an awesome spouse, or to be an understanding parent to your teenager. With all the different characteristics of life, and no owner's manual, it becomes hard to know whether or not you're on track. There are times when your Fridays feel like Mondays or your Tuesday is actually Wednesday.

> *It's common to feel like you're the only one facing your issue, but it's not the truth.*

Have you ever been in a place where you're trying extremely hard and for some odd reason nothing is coming together?

After experiencing an above average degree of success as a professional network marketer, I developed the confidence and belief that I could continue having success in business. From 2009 to 2015, I launched five different startups and none of them were successful. By successful, I mean having a positive cash flow. During this time period, my family suffered economically.

My wife and I were under a tremendous amount of stress from bill collectors, and from our debts to friends and family. People were willing to help financially because they believed in me and my vision. But it seemed like no matter what I did, nothing would work. I invested long hours in research and development on my projects. I took the time to evaluate my business plans closely, and I even sought outside counsel. Still, no favorable results. Based on what I saw; it had become pretty obvious to me that I wasn't as good in business as previously thought. I had a wife, three children, and no income to support them. It was rough. I searched for jobs and had a few interviews, but no success there either. I began to fill my mind with negative thoughts about who I was as a person. "Maybe," I thought, "I've been living an unauthentic life."

There were many people counting on me to succeed, and the pressure had become unbearable. It got to the point where I just wanted to take my bat and ball and walk away. I really didn't know what to do at this point. My wife gave me a solution that completely turned everything around. She asked me to rely on God. This was an idea I had not considered. I knew He was there, but I didn't know how to engage Him. Now came the time when I really had to build a true relationship with Him.

So, what do you do when you need to learn something new? You go to YouTube. There's where I began to listen carefully to Bishop T.D. Jakes. His influence helped me create an unbelievable relationship with my God, and there were awesome praise songs that encouraged my spirit. You may have a different view on spirituality, and you may pray differently. My only advice is that you find someone or something that is bigger than you to place your faith in. Once I began to make the shift, I was able to take the burden off my shoulders and place it in God's hands. This action allowed me to experience peace, something I hadn't felt in years. There comes a time when you realize that you've done all you can do. At that point, there are certain key characteristics you will naturally develop from this process.

The first is faith, your ability to expect and believe in what has not yet come to pass. Unwavering faith is hard, because you want to believe that what you're seeing is real. You go to your mailbox and there are past due bills, collections agencies are calling your phone seven to ten times per day, and your bank account is constantly in and out of the negative. At this point, you might be asking yourself, "Am I supposed to believe that my future will be bright and prosperous?" Absolutely. I began to see that this was only a test, and not my true reality. Whatever you're going through right now is a test, and because you picked up this book, you will learn that you now have the answers to your test.

The second key characteristic is patience. The seed has been sown, and you've assumed responsibility to nurture and protect it, but you can't be certain when the seed will take root. You must wait patiently for the harvest, and there is no definite time frame to see the yield. Your patience will be tested. This is all in hopes that you will speak death to the seed, or depart from nurturing it. You may have planted a seed for financial increase, better health, or better relationships. Maybe you planted seeds for all of the above. You have to remember, this will lead to a life of purpose and happiness, and the enemy doesn't want you to have this. Don't be fooled by his tricks or delusions.

Childlike Forgiveness

There's no question that children are God's greatest gift to man. Their youthfulness and exuberance is always awesome to see. Children have a way of reminding you of what's important in life, no matter the challenges or obstacles you may be going through. Children remind you that your problems aren't that bad. They are really great at teaching you how to handle problems.

Have you ever noticed how resilient they are? They don't hold on to the past like adults do. As a parent, I never enjoyed having to discipline my children. All three of my children are blessed with an immense capacity for forgiveness. I think about the times I had to raise my voice and use a stern tone, or when I had to send them to their bedroom for a timeout. My middle child despised going to his room, and would get tremendously upset while making his way there. Within minutes, he could come out of that room with a smile on his face and displaying a love that was pure. It always amazes me that they are able to shake off their negative emotions and return to loving emotions so quickly. It also amazes me that, as adults, we hold onto those negative emotions for so long. This leads to lifelong negative stories that we keep in our heads.

Children master the law of forgiveness. This is a biblical law, so its effectiveness cannot be denied. I want you to take time this week to address people you have not forgiven. I think it's time to make a choice, a choice to forgive and release the pain because it's time to move on. We can follow the lead of our little gifts from God, our children, who have shown us the power of forgiveness, and how healthy and refreshing it can be. As you become stronger, forgiveness will happen faster. Soon, you will be a master of forgiving.

Someone Else's Perspective

Another way to gain purposeful perspective in life is through reading about others who overcome great odds to succeed. When your life isn't heading in the right direction, a great course correction can come from the experience of others. When I felt like I was a total failure in business, I would go online and research self-made billionaires. By studying their biographies, I was able to take a glance into the past and follow their stories. There were two common denominators among all the billionaires I researched: they failed consistently, and they had an innate ability to withstand enormous emotional pain.

If we could look into the future to make corrections today, it would be easy to avoid our mistakes and learn lessons. Unfortunately, we can't. We do, however, have access to other people's journeys, from which we can learn a great deal. Be cautious though, you should never get advice from people who are not where you want to be. You naturally want to consult with friends that you trust, love, and care about. The problem with this is that you might take on bad information from people who aren't proven in a particular area. My mother provided one of the most amazing childhoods any kid could ever ask for. Any and everything my heart desired was given to me with total love. My mother also believed in spending money happily. She wasn't concerned about saving any money. I got my first job at the local supermarket, and began to earn my own income.

Unsurprisingly, I followed in my mother's footsteps. I would get paid on Friday morning and be broke on Friday afternoon, but I was happy. I had no concept of financial responsibility. As I got older, I saw that I needed to understand that concept. That revelation came by being around financially accountable people. My mother wasn't financially responsible. It's normal to want to ask someone you trust for advice. She would've given me advice to the best of her ability, and that advice would have led me to financial challenges. Today, I am able to help educate and assist my mother financially as a result of taking advice from the right people.

Billionaire Oprah Winfrey was born into poverty in rural Mississippi, to a teenage single mother. Raped at age nine and pregnant by age fourteen, Oprah had a rough childhood. Her baby died in infancy, and she was sent to live with a barber in Tennessee. Today, she calls him her father. While still in high school, she landed a job co-anchoring an evening radio show. Because of her emotional IQ, she eventually got moved to daytime television. Oprah is now worth an estimated $3 billion. Reading her biography was of great value to me. It provided clarity and, most importantly, inner belief. No matter what struggle you may encounter, there's always someone who was faced with a greater struggle and overcame it.

It's common to feel like you're the only one facing your issue, but it's not the truth. There is nothing new under the sun. This means that you can find a way out of any problem you have and become victorious.

Jay-Z happens to be one of my all-time favorite artists. Through his music, he paints a vivid picture of going from struggle to success. As a young man, this inspired me. When I learned what he overcame to succeed, it took my respect to a whole new level. Shawn "Jay-Z" Carter was born in Brooklyn, New York. He grew up in Marcy projects, one of New York's poorest communities. He was raised by his mother and has three siblings. Their father left them when he was twelve, and I remember Jay-Z discussing the impact this had on him as a young man. His environment required him to be tough and intuitive. His childhood was filled with the sound of gunfire. Before he was ten, he'd seen people shot.

With no father figure in his life, he turned to the neighborhood doughboys for guidance. They were the ones that represented success in his neighborhood. They had the knots of money, gold chains, and hot whips. Jay-Z did not graduate from high school. Instead, he took his intelligence into the cocaine game. His mother remembers him banging on pots and pans, and, as he got older, rapping to beats on his boom box. It would drive his family crazy. Today, Jay-Z is one of the all-time best-selling rap artists, selling more than 100 million records and winning twenty-one Grammys. Jay-Z's net worth exceeds $500 million, making him one of hip hop's wealthiest moguls.

Bronx native Jennifer Lopez was born into a relatively poor family. She attended Catholic schools for the majority of her education, and she found a passion for song and dance. In school, she excelled more athletically than academically. Her family stressed the importance of having a strong work ethic. Despite her talent, her parents attempted to tear down her dreams by telling her that it would be a stupid idea to pursue those goals. She pushed past their advice to follow her dreams, and today she's one of Hollywood's most successful entertainers. She truly represents the American dream.

During my season of fighting failed attempts, I was introduced to Mr. Tyler Perry. Tyler Perry is best known for his plays about a crazy black matriarch by the name of Madea. These plays, which he wrote, directed, produced and starred in, were a tremendous success. It appeared that Tyler had come out of nowhere; he was an overnight success. I learned about his journey from an interview on *Oprah*.

Tyler was born in New Orleans, Louisiana to a father, mother, and with three siblings. Tyler described his childhood as a nightmare. He was beaten and molested frequently until the age of ten. As a child, he attempted suicide in order to get away from his father. Tyler did not graduate from high school, but he did go back to get his GED. Writing and acting became therapeutic for him, and allowed him to express his emotions in a productive way. Tyler attempted to get his first play off the ground for three consecutive years. He saved his money, invested it in the play, and did it all over again when the play failed.

Finally, he had a show that became a major success. Perry knows his success was through the grace of God. This was the turning point that led him to become one of Hollywood's most successful moguls. Tyler's movies have done more than $1 billion in sales. He mastered getting a large box office return on a small budget. He now has an estimated net worth of over $400 million. Tyler Perry is living proof that no matter how great the struggle, the outcome can still be greater.

If you're looking for hope and inspiration, read some of your favorite athletes, entertainers, or entrepreneurs biographies. Their bios can provide clarity and hope during a dark time. These are just a few of the biographies I read when I was flat broke and nothing was working. I chose to read their stories rather than watch their movies or listen to their songs because they helped me see a pattern.

All successful people who take the road less traveled share a combination of attributes. It doesn't matter if it's Jennifer Aniston, Jim Carrey, or Will Smith. By reading their bios, you can learn the keys to their success and unlock some of the closed doors in your life. Now you can unlock the potential of your finances or your relationships. If you want a successful marriage, talk to people who've been happily married for twenty-five years. If you want to become a multi-millionaire, get to know a multi-millionaire and ask them to mentor you. Whether you want to be a lawyer or doctor, it doesn't matter; you need to get perspective and information from those who've achieved in this area.

Statistically, none of the people I mentioned should have achieved the level of success they are now experiencing. What was it that allowed them to defy the odds? Some of the success stories you will learn about will challenge all the excuses you might have. They didn't have mentors or business coaches for support. In fact, they were forced to figure it out with very little guidance.

Now that we are in the information age, we don't have to figure it out. You can reduce your struggle and shorten the time frame to success by utilizing other people's perspective and experience. Use online resources to help you get prepared for advancement.

In the next chapter, I'm going to show you how to take your vision and turn it into results. You've figured out what you want, but now you have to take the necessary actions to accomplish your quantum leap. Throughout this book, I've taken you through my personal experiences to better equip you to utilize this information. Now it's time to hop in the Bugatti of life, and put the pedal to the metal.

Law 4: Empowerment

You must fuel progress:

When you obtain new knowledge, skills, and philosophies, the worst thing you can do is not put what you know into action. Empowerment is: what to do + how to do it + why you do it. You must put these new skills to test, evaluate your outcome, and adjust when necessary.

Visualize escaping from the struggle; it is
different than wishing it was over.

Chapter 12:

Outcome Focused

Imagine Your Desired Ending and Start There

I think it's safe to say that we all are faced with different types of struggle. Struggle is designed to arm you with wisdom and provide lessons for further growth. But the question is what will your outcome from this lesson be. Most people believe the struggles they're facing won't change. Change happens whether you want it to or not, but progress is different. Progress is advancement in your life, which may or may not occur. Through choices and actions, you can change the direction of your struggle and have a better outcome.

Are you willing to do what's necessary to yield the outcome you want for your life? I think you are, because you chose to pick up *The Art of the Struggle.* You want to be better armed to master your struggle. Most people are unable to shift the direction of their struggle because they never visualize themselves escaping it.

Visualize escaping from the struggle; it is different than wishing it was over. Most people want the pain to go away quickly. You have to visualize the end of your struggle daily. The outcome needs to be your *Struggle de Picasso.* Beautiful and exciting, when you think about it, regardless of your emotional state, it puts a smile on your face. Emotion is the octane to your fuel. Try each day to keep your thoughts productive.

Do you want a greater spiritual connection? Are you seeking monetary benefits? Perhaps something lifestyle related? These are all questions you have to ask yourself. Really take the time to deeply consider, then decide what is most important to you. Until there is a sincere desire for transformation, you will continue on your current course. Each year will be a repeat of the last. 2016 will be the same as 2009. Decide now that this is it, and refuse to do it all over again.

I recognized that I had to strengthen my relationship with God. It may be something different for you. I knew that I needed someone on my side to help me through this tough time. Since God is all knowing, the beginning and the end, He was the one most qualified to help. I really recommend practicing spirituality. I had to do a better job trusting and relying on God to assist me in solving my problems. I was a do-it-yourselfer (or an overly confident egomaniac), and felt indestructible. I thought all my success was due to my efforts. I gave no glory or praise to God. When I attempted to use that same strategy to fix my problems, there weren't any results. It soon became clear that I wasn't the reason for my excellence, or my success. God lent me favor, and converted my action into results. If you misuse your favor, He can take it back.

You may need a specific amount of money to turn your situation around. If that money were to come to you today, would you be a good steward of it? Many times, the problem isn't a lack of money, but the way someone handles the money that they have. People believe that money will be the answer to their problems, but it won't. Often, it's a catalyst for bigger problems.

Think about how you will reward yourself for achieving something great. Where will you go? What will you do? Who will you celebrate it with? How will you live when there are no limits on your life?

You might have noticed that I didn't use the word "would" in my questions. I used "will," because you have everything inside of you to make it real. There is zero doubt in my mind.

I don't believe there's a single person who grows up and decides to be average. Did you ever say, "I want my success to be mild?" Do you want your success to be an inspiring example to others? I believe that the struggle wears many down emotionally, and causes them to settle for convenience. It's a devastating mistake. In Chapter Seven, I discussed the reason vision is a principle of success. Your eyes can lie to you, and make you believe your current situation is your permanent situation. You have to imagine yourself two or three years from now; what does it look like? I'm not asking you to daydream, but I am asking you to spend more time constructing your future. Otherwise, you'll destroy your future by holding onto the past.

Distractions are some of the biggest thieves of achievement. Sometimes they're trivial and sometimes they're enormous, but they have a way of getting you unfocused. The more you lose focus, the more wasted time is compounded. By the time you recognize it, you will be well into your later years. What are some contributing factors that keep you distracted? Be honest with yourself, you'll never progress if you continue to lie to yourself.

> *Inspiration comes from within; it isn't anything someone can give you.*

What is distracting you currently? What have you allowed to earn your focus? Is it your environment, gossip, entertainment, technology or undesirable circumstances? You have the ability to change this. I think people want to stay focused, but fail to realize the power they have given their distractions. There are producers and consumers. Distractions are the ultimate consumer of time, energy, and money. Let's think about how much time you spend in front of the television. If you were as consistent in working on yourself as you are in watching your favorite shows, your destructive struggle would cease to exist.

For some people, it's so bad that they rush home and schedule their life around their favorite shows or games. I'm not saying entertainment is terrible, but too much of it can run your life. When you take a personal inventory of the amount time you invest each week in television, it may be alarming. The average American watches four to five hours of television each day. That's almost thirty hours per week. For some people, that's more time than they spend at their jobs.

Is your relationship a distraction? Is your significant other adding value or taking away value? If you're married and your spouse is a distraction, I'm not suggesting that you get divorced, but you can learn how to manage them as a distraction. Is your spouse unsupportive of your vision or dream? They may not be to blame for feeling the way they do, especially if there were some major failures in the past. If that's the case, you shouldn't demand their support until you've proven your vision with results. Do you have a needy spouse? The key here is going be time management. You are going to have to make sure to carve out enough time for them in your week. Do this, and you'll show them how important they are to you, despite the fact that you're pursuing success intensely. It's really important to make sure there is a place at home you can find peace when you're working hard to get out of the struggle. Zig Ziglar calls it, "your home court advantage."

I believe remaining focused is even more important than getting focused. This journey will take time and patience. First, you need to be inspired. Inspiration comes from within; it isn't anything someone can give you. You have to seek out aspects of life that inspire you. A keynote video, or book could trigger inspiration. You may need a vision board of all the things that you want to accomplish in the future. Once you establish the things that inspire you, the next step is consistency. You have to keep the images and voices regularly in front of your eyes and ears. I recommend establishing several reasons why you need to accomplish your vision. You're going to need leverage on yourself to see permanent change. The best way to place leverage on yourself is to establish several reasons why you need your vision to materialize. Take the time right now to write down five reasons, and keep those reasons in your car, on the bathroom mirror, and cell phone home page.

Developing new habits can be easy. One of my mentors taught me a lesson that has aided me through the years. I'd been on my growth regimen since 2010. He said, "A wise man knows when to no longer trust a routine that doesn't bear fruit". If you watch TV much more than you read, try the opposite. Read more books that are designed to help you become better. Instead of five hours of TV per night, reduce it to two. You don't have to give up television, just shift the ratio of entertainment to education. If you buy gossip magazines, try business and educational magazines. If all your friends are broke, make some friends who are experiencing success in their life. If you eat bad food all day, try eating good food. If you're always pursuing blondes, try brunettes. If you make a conscious effort to change your habits by doing the opposite, you will begin to receive the opposite of what you are currently getting. If what we are currently getting is not what we really want, then we have to make adjustments to produce different activities that will yield different results.

You cannot compromise; be non-negotiable about your life. Your life matters, not just to you but to everyone around you. So, no more games. It's time to get serious about taking your life to an extraordinary place. Next level thinking will produce next level outcomes. You have to remember that you can't follow your feelings. Instead, you have to follow your focus. Trust me when I say that you are going to make some mistakes along the way.

It can be challenging to trust a complete stranger to lead you on a journey you've never taken before, but you do it every time you get on an airplane. Have you ever asked for documentation on the pilot before boarding the plane? And even though we don't know who he is, we trust the school bus driver with our children. Why do we trust so easily? Because we rely on brand recognition, and we trust that these companies have vetted their employees properly. But we know very little about the people running those companies. Somehow, everything seems to work out. You have to trust this information the same way.

With over a decade of experience and results, I've demonstrated the ability to help others alter their futures. I'm providing the blueprint, but you need to do the work. Together, we can create something epic in your life. Just keep saying, "Do the opposite, get the opposite," throughout this process. This isn't about perfection, it's about discipline, consistency, and effort. When you feel the urge to watch the playoff game, grab a book. If your favorite song comes on the radio, put on an insightful audiobook instead.

The decision to change your life is a seed. When you plant the seed, you have to nurture and protect it from harsh weather. You have to water your seed and pull the weeds from the garden every day. Growing as a human is the same: it requires attention every day. There are no days off, no setbacks and no breaks. Ladies and Gentlemen, it's go time!

There's a little person inside of each and every one of us who wants to have fun, be fulfilled, and explore new possibilities.

Chapter 13:

"Why?" The End Game

Transformation Starts with Your Why

Why have people like Dr. Martin Luther King, Steve Jobs, and President Barack Obama inspired millions for generations? What sets these individuals apart from the rest of us? There are many great orators similar to Dr. King. We've also seen great inventors who created products that reshaped our technological world. There are many great African American leaders who left their mark on this planet, but why was Barack Obama the first to make it into the White House? What separates these three individuals from all the rest? It's their "why?" their purpose, that differentiates them from all others. Whether you recognize it or not, the life you currently live was inspired by your "why?" It's pretty simple to understand: purpose drives behavior, behavior induces action, and action leads to results. In this chapter, you are going uncover your deep "why?" - the one that scares you, and the one that could inspire countless lives around the world.

"Why?" Discovery

Network marketing positioned me to meet thousands of people from all walks of life. I've had the privilege to meet and listen to people from all seven continents. A common trait that almost all of them shared was an inability to find their true purpose. Finding your purpose can be quite challenging.

When we're in school, we're not taught the formula for authenticity. We've been instructed to follow the leader, which leads us to feel that we've been living a lie. Our lives are nowhere close to the ones we were called to live. Most of us work at jobs we hate, and live in communities we never imagined ourselves occupying. Why is being real so hard?

After listening to thousands of stories, I came to the conclusion that most people have lost sight of their inner child. There's a little person inside of each and every one of us that wants to have fun, be fulfilled, and explore new possibilities. We tend to mute this voice, and replace it with the voice of logic and reasoning. I've yet to meet a person who reasoned or analyzed their way to superstardom or magnificent success. Often, those who follow their instincts are considered crazy people. I know my family thought I was crazy for deciding not to pursue medicine.

I have personally fallen victim to ignoring that childlike voice in my head. Over the past four years I have had this constant egging on to write a book and become a professional motivational teacher on human transformation. As a professional network marketer, I was already doing some of the work. Helping people take themselves from where they were and showing them a plan to get to where they want to be. I thought I was getting out of line with my *calling* and *purpose*. To go off and do something on my own was audacious. I had moments of great inspiration, focus, and desire. Somehow, I would suppress these emotions, then set them aside. Over the past four years there was this internal fight, yearly, to begin or wait. I came up with elaborate excuses why I couldn't write a book, or start a new website, or begin marketing myself appropriately without interfering with my current business. I felt stuck and frustrated at the same time.

What has your heart been yearning for? What should you really be doing? I remember listening to great personal development leaders from *Success Magazine*. They were conversing about the importance of being true to yourself. I had to honestly ask myself if I was being real. It was tough to admit to myself that I wasn't. It was obvious that I wasn't in a place of happiness or true fulfillment. I think most people have the ability to recognize this in themselves. It's easy to know if something is a right fit for you or not. How do you discover what it is that you're truly here to do?

You have to begin by tracing your happiest moments back to your childhood. I want you think about what you truly enjoyed doing. Back then, you probably were doing it for free. If you had the opportunity to interview some old childhood friends, how would they describe you? What was your claim to fame? Even if you were a troublemaker, there was likely a positive essence about you through all the trouble you caused. How would your elementary and junior high teachers describe you? I highly recommend that you take the time to go back to people in your life and ask them these questions. This, I know for a fact, is where the secret of what you were truly called to do is hidden.

I was a very active child growing up. I played sports, caught animals for my private pet store, and enjoyed building things. My friends and I built treehouses and teepees out of scraps from around the yard. Demolition was a big part of our summers. Based on this information, I would honestly think there's an engineering or construction personality inside me. There was a time I wanted to work in construction. But those are merely the things that I enjoyed doing for fun and excitement. They did not give me purpose or lasting satisfaction.

When I was around twelve, I discovered what truly gave me purpose, inspiration, and joy. It was a natural calling. My friends called me Pastor Reg, and looking back, I can see why I got that nickname. I loved providing wisdom and counsel. I was given this nickname not because I was preaching the gospel, but because I could listen to and encourage others with a natural ease. I would have conversations into the wee hours, helping my friends with relationship, family, and financial issues. I noticed that I could operate in this space for hours without feeling fatigued or tired. No matter how the conversation went, I would get off the phone feeling full of life. Eventually, I understood this was my "why?" It's my life's work, and I plan to do it well.

I'm pretty sure if you took the time to look back at your childhood, then fast forward to this very moment in time, you will find core characteristics that are aligned with the real you. These personality traits really defined who you were growing up. As elementary as it may seem, this exercise will help you remember what inspired you, gave you purpose, and kept you happy. What is most alarming, or the shocking part, is when you realize how far off track the real you has gotten; because of societal influences. But it's okay. Just like me, you also have the ability to turn everything around and begin to head in the right direction.

> *...excuses are nothing more than an argument for your limitations – and when you argue for your limitations, you get to keep them.*

Honing Your "Why?"

Rationally, it's pretty easy to come up with a "why?" or a purpose to pursue. What's not easy is honing and harnessing the power from the "why?" that stimulates continuous motivation. You can find many reasons to transform, but there will only be a few that cause you to act. It can be your children, your spouse, or maybe even a loved one who is in dire need of your help. There are a million reasons why you should change your life. The biggest challenge is identifying the right one. You have to find a deep, strong "why?" to move and inspire yourself to take the proper action. It almost needs to be selfish and crass to truly to get you to do what it is you're supposed to do.

Let's assume that your health is at risk and you truly need to get in better shape. In this case, being in good health for your children is your "why?" for exercising and eating healthier. But if this is the only reason you give yourself for losing weight, it won't provide enough leverage on you.

If instead, you decided that you wanted to lose twenty pounds because you would feel sexier in your bathing suit, your significant other would be more attracted to you, and you wanted to be here as long as possible for your children, you'd be talking the talk to achieve this goal. It's time for you to make this happen in your life. And when you do, you'll inspire others. It's truly remarkable. You will be able to walk them through the same process that allowed you to change your life.

This is why I am excited about helping people learn the art of the struggle. I'm on a mission to inspire others to share testimonies of the struggle that held them from their true destiny. Simon Sinek, author of the New York Times bestseller *Start with Why* says something very profound in his TEDx talk: "People don't buy what you do, they buy why you do it." Your friends and family around you are counting on you to be the change agent; the person that breaks down the walls of lack and delay and opens new doors for wealth and prosperity.

Theodore Roosevelt said, "Failure is an opportunity to begin more intelligently."

Chapter 14:

Massive Action

Time to Put in the Work

In the Bible, there is a story known as The Parable of the Ten Minas.

A nobleman was preparing to leave his house for a distant country. He gathered ten of his servants, and told them he would be leaving for some time. The nobleman gave each of his servants ten minas (an ancient unit of currency) and asked them to put his money to work until he returned. When the nobleman returned, he summoned his servants to find out what they did with the money he gave them. The first servant came before him and said, "Sir, my mina has made ten more minas." The nobleman said to him, "Well done, you are a good servant." Because he was found faithful, his master gave him authority over ten cities. The second servant was called, and said that his mina had made five minas. The nobleman was pleased, and gave this servant authority over five cities.

The third servant came saying, "Sir, behold, here is thy mina, which I kept hidden in a napkin: for I was afraid of you, in fear you were a severe man. You withdraw what you did not deposit and reap what you did not sew." The nobleman said to him, "I will judge you by your own words, you wicked slave! So, you knew did you, that I was a severe man, withdrawing what I didn't deposit and reaping what I didn't sow? Why then didn't you put my money in the bank, so that when I returned I could have collected it with interest?" And he said to his attendants, "Take the mina from him, and give it to the one who has ten." But they said to him, "Sir, he has ten minas already!" The nobleman replied, "I tell you that everyone who has, will be given more, but from the one who does not have, even what he has will be taken away."

You must couple your vision to your purpose, convert both from inner thoughts and emotions to outward expressions. This will demonstrate what you've learned, and how you implement it in your life.

The third servant in the parable listened to the wrong people, the commoners, and allowed them to rob him of opportunity. Jim Rohn, in discussing the Parable of the Sower, mentioned that sometimes the birds get the good seed that is thrown. This servant allowed the birds to take his seed. He took no action, and so he reaped no reward. This a perfect illustration of accepting advice from people who are not qualified to give it. He became immobilized, and without action there could be no achievement. Stop allowing people's opinions to have power over your life. How much opportunity have you missed out on because of the birds?

There are so many amazing people who've read all the right books and invested money into the very best seminars, but still haven't achieved their dreams or fixed their problems. Have you heard it said that information is power? If information were power, then everyone would be living their life at the highest level. All information does is prepare you, or provide you with potential power. It's your responsibility to take that potential and make it actual.

Remember, the three servants around the nobleman all received the same information, mentorship, and coaching. Two of the servants took action, while the third did not implement his training. The third servant, though he was given the same information as the other two, did not see positive results. If you understand this parable, you know exactly what you need to do. Be careful of the birds in your life, they're always looking to gobble up the seeds you receive from this book.

In order to completely transform your life, you have to take massive action on a continual basis. You cannot be casual with this decision. You must totally engage and surrender to this philosophy. Some people casually attempt to change their lives, and never get the result they're looking for. I've heard it said that if you treat your business, relationships, or health - casually, you will eventually become a casualty.

If you start a business, what is it going to take for you to launch that business in a big way? First, it's going require astute preparation. I'm talking about hours upon hours of research, learning, and formalizing a business plan. This activity alone could take you weeks, possibly even months. Once you understand the industry you're entering, and what your target market (it) there comes the legal work of filing and getting documentation. After that, there's securing proper funding, and planning. Depending on what industry you choose, you may have to identify a brick and mortar location. This involves lease negotiation, utility costs, and human capital costs. After that, you have to work on the branding aspects of your business, from stationery to brand messaging. You will need to hire a digital design artist to help you create your website. To help ensure your success, you also have to cultivate mentorship and support.

All these things will have to be done before you even engage with the customer. You may have to find time for all of this while maintaining a full-time job and a family. It's very likely that you'll go through a learning curve, and experience massive failure on your way to success. You have to stay determined – the journey through this jungle requires intense, daily action. It doesn't matter whether you're trying to lose weight or better your financial situation, compounded effort over time is the only thing that's going to help you change it all around.

Results Based Education

Being busy is nothing new. I often meet people who are extremely busy, whose schedules are always full and leave them with very little time to do what they enjoy. The crazy part of this mentality is that they are no closer to their dreams than they were five years before. Why? Because most people don't understand that it's not productive to just be busy. When it comes to productivity, it yields a predictable result, based on a specific effort compounded over time. Being busy yields no predicted result over time. They both require effort and energy, but one takes you forward and the other keeps you going in circles. Let's focus on being more productive. Productive people feel that they have time because they are doing what they enjoy doing. Once you become productive in your goal seeking activities, then you can prepare for the next lesson associated with results.

> *If you treat your business, relationships, or health - casually, you will eventually become a casualty.*

Welcome to Failureville! Progress and failure are joined at the hip; when you produce results, not all of them will be successes. Failure is not an indication that you are not doing the right thing and should quit. On the contrary, the greater and more numerous your failures, the greater your rewards will be. My mentor once told me that the person who fails the most, ultimately becomes the most successful. For everything that goes wrong there's going to be the opportunity, going forward, for you to do it better. Your attitude is going to make the difference. Your interpretation of your failures will deeply impact the speed of your continued actions.

Here's a great example: I have two sons, ages two and three. I pay very close attention to how they respond to adversity, and how they learn from it. When they were learning to walk, both boys fell down and bumped their heads frequently. I watched them keep trying over a sustained period of time, and even learn from their previous experience – they tended to avoid areas of the home where they fell or hit something. Alex, my youngest, once tried to walk forward down the stairs. He fell flat on his face, screamed and cried and was really hurt. The next day, he wanted to go down the steps again. This time, though, he turned around, got on his knees, and crawled backward down the steps because he knew he was not capable of walking down them yet.

Lance Armstrong said, "Pain is temporary – quitting last forever." Would my children have learned how to walk without consistent effort? And why did they believe that they could walk to begin with? It's because they saw other people walking. You have to have the same attitude about your life. You have to know that you're going to go from crawling, to walking, to running someday soon. And how do I know that? Because, I see so many around us, running at great speeds. I know that you can, too.

For some reason, adults have the hardest time understanding this simple concept. But, if you can force yourself back to this place, your struggle will come to an end. You have to be willing to become a student again. I taught this to all my leaders throughout the country. When you're learning something new, you must expect to make mistakes. The learning begins during these mistakes. If everything worked out perfectly, you'd never have the opportunity to learn and mature.

I worked very hard in school. Sometimes it paid off, and sometimes it didn't. If I received a bad grade in high school, I knew I had another opportunity to study and do better on the unit test. What would have happened if I quit school the first time I received a bad grade? Sounds pretty wild, doesn't it? Your current reality is a direct reflection of your best thinking thus far. It's going to require some help, plus new information and trial and error to correct the errors in the past. Hopefully, through my perspective I can help compress your timeframe.

Action Limiters

I want to talk you about a few things that limit action, and how you can avoid them. The first action killer is procrastination. We have all been subject to stalling from taking action in our lives. Procrastination is nothing more than doing less pleasurable activities after your more pleasurable activities. This means that the things we need to do, may never get done. The common mistake here is your association with discipline and pleasure.

As I mentioned earlier, you're going to dodge anything you associate with pain. It's a good strategy to trick your mind into liking the work you don't enjoy doing. Achievement involves tricking your mind to conceive and believe differently.

Getting in shape is a great example. We all know that working out can be painful when you're out of shape. When I turned thirty, I noticed some additional skin around my stomach, and that my six pack was disappearing. I knew my daily activity was low, and that I needed cardio. I chose to start running around my neighborhood block, which is a little over a mile long, five days a week. The first day out was ridiculously painful. My chest was burning and I kept spitting up something. I made it three quarters of the way and walked the rest. When I returned home, I was in shock. I used to be able to run the mile in under five minutes. I had let myself go. I was determined to crush those five days. Well, I'm not proud to say that the physical and mental pain won that first round. I made it three out of five days. We are all subject to avoiding pain. Pain is a great servant, but a terrible master.

Hopefully, this inspires you to get healthy and in shape. You can inspire yourself by watching workout videos on YouTube, or looking at your fit friends on Facebook. Say you're inspired by desperation, because a doctor told you your health is at risk. I overcame procrastination with sheer willpower; I forced myself to do what I didn't want to. I committed to doing the opposite of whatever I felt. If I needed to write my book, I would imagine the success of the book as my inspiration. I'd force myself to sit down and write one thousand words every hour. You'll have to find a way to remove the association of pain from the action you need to perform, allowing you to engage and get results.

Another limiter of action is lack of resourcefulness. Sometimes, people use what they don't have, as an excuse for why they can't be successful or achieve their goals. When you make a decision, be one hundred percent committed to your conclusion. Deciding to win comes before the game starts. Resourcefulness is the by-product of commitment and focus. Therefore, lack of money, time, or know how, are no longer action limiters. You will feel unstoppable and nothing can get in the way of you completing your task.

Let's say you live in the Midwest, and a wealthy business-person made you this offer: If you can get to California without borrowing money or taking a plane, they will pay you one million dollars. It's probably fair to say that you would do whatever it took, because you saw what the outcome from your effort would be. You'd have to be incredibly resourceful. How would you do it? Would you hitchhike and jump trains? That would be the definition of true resourcefulness.

Finally, one of the greatest action limiters is our instinctive need to make excuses. I heard an incredible man once say that excuses are nothing more than an argument for your limitations – and when you argue for your limitations, you get to keep them. So often I meet incredible people who are smothered in excuses. When you explain why you have not done, achieved, or accomplished something in your life, you are simply lowering your demands of yourself. Justification is rationalizing your excuses. Habits are not easy to break, and you must recognize your lies. Next time someone is expecting something of you and you don't deliver, observe how you respond. It's a great opportunity to learn something new about you.

The first thing you have to do is become conscious that you're making excuses. Next, you have to stop believing your excuses, because they are not real. There is nothing that you cannot accomplish if you just put your mind to it and add the proper action behind it. The moment you become excuseless, you're forced to become resourceful. How many times have you been late, and, even though it was your fault, still made an elaborate excuse? No matter what you do from this point forward, I want you to take total responsibility for it. Either you did it correctly or you didn't; there's no gray area. The moment I accepted this responsibility, everything began to move so much faster. I stopped finding excuses for my lack of success in business, lack of income, lack of time, and lack of ability. Once you get rid of the excuses, you'll be forced to grow in order to achieve more.

Sensory Acuity

Sensory Acuity is a phrase used in neuro-linguistic programming. It means being more aware of everything that is going on around you. Because you're now taking massive action, you also have to become acutely sensitive to those results. Your ability to recognize whether something is working or not is critically important. You may say, "Reggie, I am going to the gym every day and working out for three hours a day. For some reason, I'm just not losing weight." At that point, you need to recognize that something isn't working. Many people will continue ineffective patterns for an entire year. Then the new year will roll around, and they'll be disappointed that they didn't achieve their goals. You may need to go to the gym less, but watch your diet more.

Communicating with others requires sensory acuity. Have you ever known anyone who brought negative energy with them when they walked into a room? It's pretty funny that the person who causes this effect never knows they have this quality. It's even funnier if you're that person, but you notice it in someone else. That would be the ideal definition of a person who isn't acutely sensitive to their actions. It's going be important for you to improve your ability to recognize whether or not you're heading in the right direction.

"Desire is the starting point for all achievement, not a hope, not a wish, but a keen pulsating desire that transcends everything," said Napoleon Hill.

Chapter Fifteen:

Desire

What Will You Give Up in Exchange for What You Desire?

"Desire is the starting point for all achievement, not a hope, not a wish, but a keen pulsating desire that transcends everything," said Napoleon Hill. Desire is the fundamental motivation for all human action. If you sincerely seek progress, it's important for you to understand why desire is critical to your achievement. Hunger is a great example. When your appetite is curbed, you're not motivated to eat, but if you're starving there's a huge desire. How hungry are you to change your life? Your desire for change has to become greater than your fear of uncertainty. What are your desires for your life? Desires are just like a muscle group; you have to place intense demand on them to get them to stretch and tear and rebuild.

Feed Your Desire

In order for your body to sustain and renew itself, it has to be fed several times daily. Your desire for achievement also requires multiple feedings every day. Everyone's desires are different: some want freedom of time and money, others want to help others and serve their community, while still others want to make a lasting impression on the world. I'm not sure what that is for you, but what I do understand are the necessary steps to strengthen your desire, and transform it into achievement. If your desires are weak, there will be no results; if your desires are strong, the results will be strong.

My desire is to make an impact on the lives of millions. I know that this is a huge responsibility, and I had to get my desire up to the task. You may wonder how one prepares oneself to impact the whole world. You have to believe that you are worthy of the opportunity. You have to capture a vision and find some amazing people to help you make that dream a reality. Value naturally seeks other value. When you work on becoming more valuable to the world, the world will help you attract the tools and appointments needed to pursue your mission. Do you choose to accept?

When I accepted the mission to impact lives globally, there were criteria I had to meet. I had to be willing to separate myself from the pack. It was hard not being around my best friends for almost two years. I had to be careful of the conversations I had with family. Not everyone could see what I saw, and to avoid them speaking death to my vision, I had to protect it. I nurtured my vision by feeding my mind healthy information, and by surrounding myself with masterminds who were more prosperous than I.

I would spend at least one hour a day visiting my desires. I would envision my lifestyle, income, and the lives I would impact. I'd imagine how it would feel. Every single day I took a thirty minute shower. Only five of those minutes was spent washing up, the remaining twenty-five minutes was for prayer and vision exercises.

I believe I did this to protect my desire. When you are broke and struggling, your desires are volatile. By taking these long showers every day, I chose to see the future and the results. It inspired me to move forward. Eventually I developed a mental callous. Then, no matter how bad things looked, I continued to believe in and maintain my faith in my future. Life will happen, but it's your responsibility to protect your desire at all costs. Desire is the very thing you're going to need, to see the struggle cease to exist in your life. There were days when things got so bad I would take two or three showers just to be able to enter a place of tranquility.

I highly recommend that you find a desire environment in your life, whether it's your home, car, or a public facility. It doesn't take much to create an environment where you can cultivate your desire, and propel yourself to achieve what you were put here to do. You can create multiple vision boards, and situate them in different parts of your home. You could have one in the bathroom, one in the living room, one in the dining room, and another where you watch TV.

Great Achievers Have Strong Desire

Michael Jordan is undoubtedly one of the greatest basketball players of all time. When you see a list of his achievements, it's hard to believe that they could all have been done by a single man. He won six NBA championships, multiple MVP awards and appeared as an NBA All-Star for over a decade. His shoe, the Nike Air Jordan, has revolutionized the shoe industry for over two decades. And recently, Michael Jordan took majority ownership of the Charlotte Bobcats. He's also become the second African-American billionaire on the 2015 Forbes list.

But do you know about Michael Jordan's childhood? He

grew up dirt poor in Wilmington, North Carolina. He was cut from the varsity basketball team his sophomore year. What set him apart from all the other competitors on the basketball court was his desire to win. His desire was so strong that he pushed himself unlike any other player. He was looking to become the best that he could be. He didn't compare himself to John Stockton or Karl Malone, his desire was to be the best Michael Jordan he could be. One of my favorite things Jordan said is that he just wanted to be the best he could be and that is what drove him. Are you prepared to become the best you can be?

We live in a world that puts less emphasis on faith than fear.
Faith and fear are complete opposites of one another.

Chapter 16:

Faith

Stronger Faith is Required for the Journey Ahead

Do you have to see it to believe it? Do you have gladiator type faith? What does it really take to shift from little to no faith, into mega faith? It's going to require you to have an unwavering faith. Your faith cannot be shaken or deterred during this process. Enduring faith has no deadline or expiration date. Faith is knowing that something is going to come to pass that you have not yet seen or witnessed.

Faith makes me think about farmers waiting for the harvest. Being a farmer requires abundant faith. They have to trust and believe that they followed the correct steps in spring and summer, and that they will have a harvest by fall. You have to remember that this is their livelihood, and typically their only means for earning income. Farmers have faith in their land, and faith in the ground they tilled. Farmers require faith in the seeds, and how they plant the seeds in the ground. They have to have faith in their ability to cultivate the seeds, and protect them from harsh weather. Once their seeds take root, farmers have to have faith that the sun will shine throughout the spring and the summer months. The temperature of the soil and air make a difference too. They need to have faith in an adequate rain season.

Consider this. When it's time to reap the harvest, a farmer has to go into overdrive. The next sixty to ninety days, a farmer will invest anywhere from twelve to eighteen hours a day, seven days a week to make sure the harvest comes. Farmers don't sit around and wait for God. Instead, they work with God. In this process, there's very little room for error. Everything they did in the spring and the summer has to be spot-on for their harvest in the fall. There is no room for worry, doubt, or concern. They must put their faith in their ability and training to deliver predictable results. Being a farmer requires real faith. What kind of faith do you require in order to eliminate your struggle? Are you willing to put in the work needed to eliminate your struggle? Just like the farmer, you have to know without a doubt that what you see in the near future will come to pass because you've taken on the proper work ethic to create a new game plan for your life.

We live in a world that puts less emphasis on faith than fear. Faith and fear are complete opposites of one another. You can't believe both at the same time, you have to choose one. I've talked about fear, and how it's really just False Evidence that Appears Real. Whether you're worried about being late, getting sick, or not achieving your life's purpose, all of these are simply thoughts you've placed in your head. Faith is the opposite. Faith says, "I will achieve. There is nothing that can stop me. I am a conqueror and I am a victor." Faith is conditioning your thoughts to believe in the positive, and seeing the future as it's going to be, rather than how it is today. Fear will have you believe the present is actually worse than it is, so you end up speaking those fears into your future and destroying your possibilities.

Faith Impacts Your Emotions

When you travel to a new and unfamiliar destination in life, emotions are going to flare up. You'll find yourself filled with anxiety, stress, and maybe a little fear. Maybe you're taking a road trip to a new city, and your GPS system stops working. You had a whole list of thoughts that were going through your mind at the speed of light. You might wonder if you missed your turn, or if you're heading in the right direction. When something feels unfamiliar to your brain, you retreat into a defensive state. Then you get a series of thoughts that tell you to stop, turn around, and go back. Once you've gone too far, there is no turning back. The line in the sand has been drawn; the backdoor is shut. Throughout this process, you've dealt with all these different emotions. They produce unhealthy thoughts because you're feeding fear and not faith. When you're working to change your life and improve your circumstances, faith is going to play a major role in the transformation.

I want to help you realize what it feels like to be in what I refer to as "the faith zone." I used to believe I could achieve all my goals and dreams without anyone's help. I thought I was self-sufficient enough to get things done. But I quickly realized that Reggie Flowers was not enough. I've learned over the years that when you get in the place of faith, there comes a tremendous sense of peace and tranquility in your life. Let's say you wake up to a negative balance in your bank account, you find your gas tank on empty, and you only have three or four dollars in your pocket. Faith helps you believe that you have enough gas, and something will come to pass. God will make a way for you to get to work and back safely. Fear will make you worry and doubt that you won't be able to make it to work and back. But you have to choose – if you have faith in what you're doing, no matter what it is, you will be at peace throughout the process. I know this doesn't come without practice, and feeding your faith. Internally, you have to articulate to yourself that this is a challenge for you to overcome. That it's just an illusion to get you on track for achieving your ultimate goal.

The moment you begin to outsmart your fear; you begin to take complete ownership of your thinking process. Once you have control of your thinking process, you become the captain of your ship. You can charter whatever course you like, in whatever time frame you want – it's all up to you.

It's important to understand how to direct your emotions, because your emotions ultimately guide your motivation. Over time, your motivation will become discipline. Discipline will cement behavior into habit. Think about those days when your mind tells you to go for it, but your body says, "No Way." What keeps you in bed is how you feel, not so much what you thought.

Faith provides you with an emotional environment in which to achieve success. Patience, peace, and focus are all products of faith. Trusting in everything you've learned up to this point, along with believing in your ability to implement these strategies correctly, is going to require a strong faith. Skills will be needed, no question about it. But, most importantly, it's the faith that you need to do what you set out to do.

Law 5: Elevation

Growth impacts everything around you:
When you are intentional about your growth, everyone and everything around you are positively affected.

Whether you believe it or not, and whether you agree with it or not, the fact is, we feel the need to meet our peers' expectations.

Chapter 17:

Growth

Everything You Desire is Outside of Your Comfort Zone. You Must Grow to Expand it.

Did you know that you are infinitely capable of achieving any goal? You have been ordained by our amazing Father in heaven to be a conqueror on earth. This alone guarantees your success for achieving your goals and dreams. And if it were no longer a secret to you, and you knew exactly what to do, would you sincerely do it? What if this one thing required you to work on it ten minutes every day? Do you know what that one thing is? It's your ability to grow internally as a human being, to get out of your comfort zone and reach beyond what you're currently comfortable with. Long ago, my mentor said, "You have to be willing to give up stuff to go up." If you want to alter your path, sacrifice is required.

You may wonder how you'll grow. This isn't a physical trait, it's mental. Your capacity to go beyond the walls of your mental box are infinite. Society tells you that your lot in life is to be average. I want you to know, that's not true. We have the capacity to grow beyond our greatest imagination. The mind has infinite capability. It's important for you not to be fooled by you. Once the mind stretches, it cannot return back to its original state. Let's go over a few steps on exactly how to grow into your goals.

Growth Must Be Intentional

Growth doesn't happen by accident. It won't happen because you want or need it to. Growth won't take place in your life because you're getting older. You have to become intentional in your personal growth and growth areas. Intention is the fertilizer for your growth. For example, if you choose to be a better spouse, some growth areas may include: listening skills, interpersonal skills, and conflict resolution skills. These areas are not going to improve themselves, it doesn't work that way. Your growth areas may need to be in your finances or your performance at work. It doesn't matter what you want to improve, what matters is that you implement an intentional improvement system, and follow it with consistency.

John Maxwell is undisputedly the world's authority on leadership. His books and audios have become a major influence in my life and my growth plan. In one of the speeches I sat in, I heard him mention that he has had a plan to grow every year since 1972. For more than forty-three years, John has made it his life's work to grow every area of his life. Do you think this takes work? Absolutely. But the great thing about growth is that anyone is capable of doing it. Let me share an example of my personal plan.

- Shower and prayer 6:30 AM
- Thirty minutes of cardio 7:30 AM
- Productive audios related to personal development in

my car
- Attend four growth seminars per year
- Reinvest ten percent of my earnings into personal development
- Find something to do daily that makes me uncomfortable
- Compliment one stranger a day
- Expand growth areas through research
- Read thirty minutes before bed

This is a rough outline of my yearly game plan for intentional growth. Before listening to John Maxwell, I didn't have an actual plan to grow. It's important that you develop a plan that works for you, that will force you out of your comfort zone and into growth.

Follow Those Who Grow

If you haven't detected this yet, influence plays a major role in our lives. There are so many external sources that influence our decisions, beliefs, and thoughts. As I mentioned in Chapter Ten, if you do the opposite, you will get the opposite. If you are currently following people who don't have growth plans, their natural influence will dissuade you from growing. Whether you believe it or not, and whether you agree with it or not, the fact is, we feel the need to meet our peers' expectations. I'm not asking you to get rid of all your friends; I'm asking you to pinpoint three friends, colleagues, or associates who are focused on self-improvement and can hold you accountable. This will help shield you from the masses, because the masses will attempt to get you off course.

After I made the decision to become an entrepreneur, I quickly observed some obvious differences between people I spent my time with, family and friends, and people I was learning from, mentors and coaches. My mentors placed their focus on getting better. They knew that if they wanted to achieve more, they had to become more. My thinking was like a shallow puddle prior to meeting these individuals. They had me believing that reading was an imperative and vital daily activity. Today, reading is one of my mental vitamins.

I was the guy who seemed to have everything going for him, but reading was of no value at all. I didn't enjoy reading. In college, when I majored in premed, I would use Cliff's Notes just to get the information I needed to pass my test. Reading always made me sleepy. But my mentors inspired me to fall in love with reading. It wasn't until I dropped out of college that my passion for reading blossomed.

The beautiful thing about observation is that you can make it your friend. When you do that, it provides you with opportunities to learn. I observed leading business people, and their references to specific books that helped them achieve their goals. I learned early on that leaders are readers. I concluded that if I wasn't reading, I wouldn't be achieving. Just like forcing a child to eat broccoli or brussels sprouts, I forced myself to read at least ten minutes a night for 90 days. I probably started over at least three to four times, but by the fifth time, I finally figured it out. When you see other people grow, you will believe that you can grow yourself.

> *Your gifts are designed for you to have a fun and fulfilled life doing what you love.*

Make Growing Fun

From the very moment you were conceived, God placed

gifts in your life. Typically, these gifts and abilities are the desires of your heart. It's going to take consistency for you to grow and master your gifts. And the best time is now; don't wait on some day, because that day will never come. Your gifts are designed for you to have a fun and fulfilled life doing what you love. Too often, we find ourselves heading in the direction where we were either led, or forced into. This results in resentment, anger and frustration with our lives.

The first step you want to take is to identify your gifts. Here are a few ways to know if it's a gift or not: first, you're really good at it; second, you keep finding ways to utilize it; third, you love it and probably are doing it for free.

Growing up in the Baptist Church, all my cousins and friends were in the choir. I also enjoyed music, so I joined the choir to be with them. There was a one hour practice, once a week to sing on Sunday. I would come to practice excited about the songs we were going to sing on Sunday. It seemed like everyone in the choir got a solo opportunity but me. My uncle was the choir director, and I would ask him all the time if I could have a solo. He would always tell me, "Next time, nephew." It wasn't until I was a young adult that my cousins and uncle enlightened me about my real capability. I struggled to carry a tune, but the story I kept replaying in my head was a little different. Almost a decade later, I realized that I didn't lose my ability to sing – I never had the ability to sing. Singing is not my gift. The foolish thing would be for me to continue to pursue singing, hoping to, one day, land a great opportunity. You have to be sensitive to recognize what you're good at, and what you're not. Through my experience working with thousands of people, the life games we choose to play are the games we often win.

In network marketing, one of the primary skill sets was to successfully recruit people into my organization. Recruiting consisted of people you know and people you would get to know. That was exciting to me, because I knew I could do that. Then you had to become skillful at recruiting people you didn't know. I wasn't really feeling the idea of recruiting strangers. I've always been known as a social guy, but I didn't like to start the conversation. I was awesome, though, at receiving the initiation for conversation. Early on, I was taught how to go out and initiate conversations with complete strangers, and to influence them to look at my business. This was uncomfortable for me, but my desire to succeed was greater than my fear of failure.

I had to find a way to make this fun. I learned that people enjoy being complemented. My goal was to compliment at least ten people a day, I hoped that at least half of them would engage in conversation. Some would thank me and go on about their business, while others would talk my ear off. It started to feel like a game, and became fun. My competitive nature kicked in, and I wanted to dominate the game. As I got better and developed my skills, the game shifted – I wanted to see how many people would tell me no in a day. "No" represented my ability to move through rejection. I realized I was playing a numbers game. These experiences allowed failure to no longer be an enemy, but a friend. You must make failure your friend if you're going to have fun growing. When things go wrong, find a way to laugh. It's a simple solution that will allow you to keep moving forward.

Zig Ziglar said, "You can have everything in life you want, if you will just help enough other people get what they want."

Chapter 18:

Contribution

Self-Development or Self-Fulfillment?

My self-development journey began in 2005-2006. After learning that the level of my income was going to be equal to the level of my personal growth, I was on a mission to grow as fast as I could. I wanted to achieve every single goal that I have set for myself. When I launched my network marketing business, my desire was to be the number one earner in the company by the time I was twenty-five.

Let me tell you, I put work into reading books, attending all the seminars, and continuously asking God to grant me favor. God provides what He can trust you with. I didn't think there was anything He couldn't trust me with. The irony of the situation is that the person who can't be trusted doesn't know they can't be trusted. I had ethics and integrity, so I expected that God would grant me what I wanted. As a hungry young leader, there was no question that I wanted to be great at my craft, earn a lot of money, and have influence with millions of people. But I had a lot to learn. You may be in a position where you still have a lot to learn.

Now that you understand the importance of personal growth, the question you must answer honestly is: Am I growing for self-fulfillment or self-development? They both seem very similar in thought, and probably in consideration as well. But their intent differs greatly. Self-fulfillment focuses on what you gain in your development. Self-development is about how you can impact the lives of others. I can pinpoint the exact moment I realized my personal growth was self-serving. I was a pretty hardnosed leader; in your face, direct and mildly aggressive. I cared about people and their success, but it didn't outweigh how I cared about my own success. Then people around me began to feel that I didn't care as much about their needs as I did about my own needs. There's an old saying related to building trust, "people don't care about how much you know, they know how much you care."

Honestly, I was in denial when I started hearing the complaints from my up line mentor. I couldn't understand why they would complain, as I was always available and firmly committed to their success. But now I understand: my leaders wanted to know that I cared more about their success than mine, because I was the person with the influence. I remember a mentor telling me, the first thing I should do was apologize, and I remember wondering why. She told me that leaders take full responsibility for anything that goes wrong within the organization, and give credit to anything that goes right. My philosophy was totally opposed to her advice, which is why it wasn't working. I swallowed my pride, and took her advice. By focusing on others and their success, my income quadrupled the following year. Obviously, this lesson became cemented in my psyche.

Zig Ziglar said, "You can have everything in life you want, if you will just help enough other people get what they want." The Bible says, *He who supplies seed to the sower and bread for food will supply and multiply your seed for sowing and increase the harvest of your righteousness. You will be enriched in every way to be generous in every way, which through us will produce thanksgiving to God.* The world we live in today will respond favorably to the value you add to it. So, the more people you help become successful, the more successful you will become, all because you created an outbreak of success. If you can help people around you, who are going through similar problems, you will eliminate your own problems. Giving, when you don't have anything to give, is the secret to wealth. It takes you out of a scarcity mentality into an abundant mentality. There is something within the human spirit that shifts when we give without expectation.

Let's assume that your five closest friends are broke. If that's the case, the chances are that you're broke too. If you begin to focus on solutions to help their circumstances, you will help your own circumstances as well. On a spiritual level, God rewards those who serve others with a selfless heart. On a natural level, your newfound education will allow you to apply what you taught others, to your own life.

Here are five reasons people don't contribute to others more:

1. Insecurity: They're worried about what other people are going to gain from the matter.
2. Selfishness: This type of person only cares about what benefits them.
3. Vulnerability: This type of person feels that helping others is a display of weakness.
4. Ego: They will only help people if it's their idea.
5. Fear: This person is concerned about what other people will think of them.

These traits have prevented millions of people from making an honest contribution to improving our way of life. It is important that we decide to set better examples. It has been said that people don't do what you say, they do what you do. Therefore, if you want to see a better quality of individuals in your neighborhood or city, you have to become what you expect to see. It starts with you and me.

Add Value to Others

There is an amazing feeling you get when you have the ability to help others. The work I put into my personal growth began to be noticed by others through my actions and conversations. People around me began to search for more answers to their concerns and problems. Personal growth conditions your mind to be in tip-top shape. If you lose weight, people will notice. In the same way, people will see that the level of your thinking has elevated. Once people notice that you're thinking at a higher level, they believe that information is available for them to access. They will notice, the things that used to make you mad don't make you mad anymore; problems that used to bother you will no longer bother you, and the type of people you're tracking in your life is different. This isn't the time to develop a competitive edge over your fellow man. This is the time when you reach out and pull them up and show them the way to a better lifestyle.

> *It's time to stop playing with life like it's a hobby and decide to make it your profession.*

When you begin to help other people, there are a series of questions you begin to ask yourself, subconsciously:

- How can I help?
- How can I get them to dream?
- How can I challenge them?
- How can I get them to think independently?
- How can I help them become better?
- How can I expand their vision?
- How can I help them see value in themselves?

I just want to give you a few examples of the way you will begin to think once you begin serving others. It's important for you to stand bold. By becoming living proof, you'll become someone's inspiration. You may think right now that you're not anyone worthy of imitation. Before Bill Gates created Microsoft, he wasn't someone anyone wanted to be. Before Steve Jobs came back to Apple, he was definitely someone *nobody* wanted to be. So, you may be sitting here thinking that you are someone no one wants to be. But when you grow and reach your potential, you will become someone that others want to be. It all starts with you seeing the value in you. Are you worthy of living a better life?

Can you do better? If so, why haven't you done better? It's time to stop playing with life like it's a hobby, and decide to make it your profession.

Give Without Expecting

I believe that most people give without a desire to receive. But the moment the giver is in need, they generate an expectation to be repaid for their generosity. They want to find the person they helped and remind them of what they did. They expect reciprocation. How many times have you been let down when this situation didn't work in your favor? There are certain laws that cannot be broken or forsaken. The law of sowing and reaping is a law that you want to trust and live by. The law states that if you sow good seed, you will reap a good harvest. It's also adversely true – if you so bad seed, you will reap a bad harvest. Once the seed is sown, you cannot reverse this process. Here's the challenge that people encounter frequently with this law: they believe that wherever the seed was sown is where they're going to reap a harvest. That is not true. This was another valuable lesson I had to learn.

In 2012, I received a phone call from a childhood friend. He told me that some very sharp and successful individuals would be joining our business. He said it was very important for me to fly down, from Michigan to Florida, to meet them and help them get started. At that time, he didn't know that my desire for business in this area was waning. But, because I believed in others, and in standing behind my commitments, I flew down less than a week after my son was born. Over the next few weeks, I invested time and money that I truly didn't have. I saw the value of the time I invested, and I saw that my heart wasn't invested in this project. But, when you take time away from what's most important to you, you want to see a return on your efforts.

In the natural realm, I couldn't see any return – as a matter of fact, they decided to abandon this project a few months later. One of the leaders soon informed me that they were going to return to the company that we all worked with. I acted as if I didn't care. In fact, I was torn, this is because I knew the law of sowing and reaping, and it didn't feel like I was reaping any good. I remember my wife telling me with strong confidence that one day people were going to enter my business, that someone else had sowed into, as you did for them. Twelve months later, I was informed that my old organization was going to be moved underneath me. When the group left, there were about forty people – when it returned, there were more than eight-hundred business owners and seventy-five hundred customers. That was a true testament to God's grace and favor. You have to understand that His word is law. If you just add some faith and patience, you will allow Him to work in your life. Now you become the miracle that others need to see in order to believe that greater things are possible for them.

It's important that you remember to always put others first. Don't be worried about being used or taken advantage of, because there's a greater power that has your back. Just place your focus on being grateful, and the rest will handle itself. The principle focus here is to keep growing, otherwise you'll be forced to grow, and when that happens, it tends to be painful.

Everything around you may have been affected, but the good news is that you get a second chance - with a fresh start.

Chapter 19:

New Struggle

Better You. Better Life. New Challenges to Solve

The struggle is real, and fortunately, it's not going anywhere. The good news is, that as you get better, your struggle is going to get better. I remember looking back on this journey, hoping that once I got to a place of financial and emotional stability, I could share my experience and strategies for emotional strength. I don't know what type of struggle you're undertaking, but I know that what I went through was gut-wrenching. It left me with days of cloudiness and constant fear about my life. I saw myself happy in the future, but the present was so terrible I couldn't imagine a timeframe for when things were going to get better. I'm grateful to say that, by using the Five E's, I am in an awesome space right now. I'm embarking on new journeys that allow me to achieve many more of my dreams. More than I imagined possible.

Has life's volcano erupted? If so, it's perfectly okay. There is an amazing relationship between you and volcanos. The inside of the volcano is equivalent to your mind. When the magma starts to heat up and bubble, it's just like when you've reached your breaking point. When the pressure comes to a head, it's too late for damage control. Brace yourself. The volcano erupts, and even covers the sun. The molten lava destroys everything that it touches. You get the picture; it's looking pretty bad, and everything you've worked so hard for, has now been eliminated.

When you're struggling with life, you can feel the exact same way. However, with time, patience, and faith, renewal can come. When the lava settles and dries, it turns into rich and fertile soil. Eventually, the smoke dissipates and the sun shines brightly down on the brand new landscape. In this new landscape, everything has the opportunity to be better than it was before, to produce more than it did before, and to enrich its surroundings to a greater degree than ever before.

My volcano had been dormant for some time. Finally, in 2010, the eruption took place. I tried to save everything that I had worked so hard for, but it was too late. At first, I didn't really understand why I had to experience this tragedy. Looking back, my volcano eruption was the best thing that could've ever happened to me. It forced me to grow in areas that I didn't plan to grow in. It pushed me to discern and utilize wisdom better than I could've ever asked for. When my volcano erupted, it removed everything that didn't need to be there. Sometimes you need an interruption to pull you away from what's no longer valuable. God knows our desires, and he's designed a plan around those desires. He tries to get us on track, but sometimes we need that huge eruption to get our attention. This was certainly true in my case.

Today, my businesses are stronger than they've ever been, and my brand is growing. Because of this journey, I am now able to use my experiences and gifts to help others blossom into their potential.

My mission is to better serve and equip you with the proper soil, seed, nutrients, and tools to reach and exceed your potential.

Welcome to your new life!

Conclusion

In summarizing all I have shared in this book, I realize that only reading the Five E's will not lead to a life of success and happiness. You now have the blueprint that I used during my journey through the jungle of struggle. The Five E's became my navigational system to lead me in a sound and clear direction. But if you don't take the right steps, if you don't put in a new address and desired location, this book will offer nothing more than entertainment and some additional information. I don't want this to be just another purchase, or something you add to your library. I'm going to cover what to do next, and I'm also going to cover what *not* to do next.

Let Go of the Past

Do you remember how you felt when you received new and exciting information that could help you? Of course you do. What you took away was excitement, a sense of urgency, and determination. The real question is, why doesn't it last long? Why, after only a week or two, do most people return to their old habits, philosophies, and belief systems? It's because they didn't make a decision to let go of the past. It becomes very hard to drive your car while looking in the rearview mirror. TD Jakes said something that has stuck with me. He said, "When you hold onto the past, it's at the expense of your destiny."

When you work with hundreds of people personally, you begin to recognize patterns. I'd often see people who could assimilate information and execute it effectively, but only apply what they had learned for a very short time. It's because people naturally began to measure their future based on their past. People often talk themselves out of their goals and dreams, or listen to those around them who have never achieved anything great. The worst part is that these people, who have such potential, solicit information from bad sources and then internalize it. Remember: we always look for signs that either conflict or relate to our current philosophy. Our best and most consistent thinking has led us right to where we are. You have to take in new information; information from a different source, that will lead you where you want to go.

How do you stop the commercial for failure that keeps playing in your mind? It's simple: you change the channel. You can't afford to keep telling yourself what you cannot do. You have to make a conscious decision to take your past experiences and invest them in your future. Our past failures and bad experiences should be nothing more than an instruction manual for what not to do in the future. Most people use their past experiences as anchors instead of propellers. There is a reason why it's called the past – it is not your present or your future.

Start Fresh

Let *The Art of the Struggle* be like fresh air in your lungs on a beautiful summer day. It can begin a new chapter in the book of your life. You can use the old chapters as a reference guide to help assist you in authoring the greatest journey yet. Implementing the Five E's gave me that second chance feeling. You've probably heard stories about people who've had a near death experience. Did you notice how they perceive the world differently than before? It's because they learned how to place value on the right priorities. The volcano of life may have erupted for you. Everything around you may have been affected, but the good news is that you get a second chance with a fresh start.

Teach-Ability Index

Mastering this formula will grant you the life that you truly desire. The Teach-Ability Index is your willingness to learn, multiplied by your willingness to change. I know, because you are reading this book, that you have a willingness to change. You are looking for a resource that can help you. Your reading this book tells me that you probably invest time online, and in audio and print books, assimilating information to better yourself. I applaud you for your decision and your courage to take those first steps. The other side to this formula is where people tend to fall short: the willingness to change.

You may want to change, you may even *have* to change, but the fact is that most people don't change. Most are unwilling to become a student of life again. We fight so hard to maintain who we currently think we are. If you fought equally as hard to become who you are supposed to be, you would. You can't associate pain with change. Change has to become pleasure in your mind. It can no longer be this tedious and inconvenient process that derails you from your life. It has to be looked at as the gateway to happiness, love, and success.

Urgency

It's important that you take on a now mentality. Don't over estimate the amount time you have to achieve your goals and dreams. You have to remember that time is not your friend, and it waits for no one. Time has no problem leaving you behind as you wait on it. You have to develop the attitude that you're going to stay ahead of time. You will need to learn time frame impression. By investing in growing internally, you can stay ahead of time. The beautiful part about this is, that even if you've lost ten years, you can make it up in the next twelve to twenty-four months. You now have the ability to make this timeframe a hundred times more productive, and to get a hundred times more results. Now is your time; you deserve to have a magnificent life.

Survival of the Fittest

Priorities are your lifeline. Success will always go to the person who has their priorities in the most effective order. You might have been told to get your priorities in line. To do this, you have to list your priorities in order of importance. You're going to need a priority assessment. What were your priorities before reading *The Art of the Struggle*? What changes to your order are now required to help you succeed?

You can no longer operate in survival mode, doing things out of sheer necessity. Survival mode is trying to keep everything together as it's falling apart. Use the strategies in this book to help your new plan of action. My priorities were so disordered for so long, and I didn't even know it until something went wrong. It's kind of like maintenance on your car, if you avoid the basic upkeep, soon things begin to break down. Your life isn't any different. My priorities were work, work, and more work. I thought that I could work extremely hard for three years, and restore balance afterward. I was focused so intensely on my work that I didn't see everything falling apart around me. By the time I looked up, structures in my life were crumbling.

Today, my priorities are: God, family, serving others, and everything else. By adjusting my priorities, everything else has fallen into place. On my website, www.reggieflowers.com, I cover how to autocorrect your priorities.

Be authentic. Be adamant. Be audacious.

Let's Transform the World Together!

Who do you know that needs guidance and inspiration? Send the website to ten of your closest friends.

About the Author

For more than 12 years, Reggie Flowers has immersed himself in the lives of those who are looking to improve their quality of life. He has provided a very rich, soil like environment full of strategies and solutions for creating an extraordinary life. He possesses a unique ability to implement, impact, and influence his audiences to permanently elevate their standards and expectations for their lives.

Raised by a single mother, surrounded by great friends and family, Reggie had your normal childhood growing up. He doesn't come from wealth or abundance. But, he was fortunate to be planted in good soil.

Off to college, he was introduced to a plethora of life's challenges. By the time Reggie was 20 years old he was an official college dropout and his girlfriend at the time was pregnant with his daughter. Over the past 10 years Reggie had a TV drama like series of successes and huge failures. Reggie is no different than you, he doesn't possess any talents or abilities that you don't have. He simply had a strong enough belief and desire to achieve what he felt he deserved.

Now, millionaire entrepreneur, blossom strategist, re-nowned author, husband and father of three wonderful children; Reggie Flowers thoroughly knows what it takes to overcome adversity and personally transform your life. As a business, finance, and relationship expert, Reggie has forged a unique path for those who need help in any area of their lives.

Regardless of the struggles that may be holding you back from achieving your desired life, Reggie's unmatched strategies will allow you to break free and realize your dreams. He has transformed the lives of thousands all over the world through webinars, conference calls and live events. His passion is felt by others as he equips and empowers them with the knowledge and skills to manage their emotions, the art of transformation, and living fulfilled lives.

Reggie is a sought after mentor and consultant with exceptional results with private and publicly traded, multi-level marketing companies. His deepest expertise is in leadership development, organizational performance, brand development, and customer, distributor acquisition. His experience in distribution strategy, relationship marketing and trend evaluation is extensive.

Reggie is chairman and founder of Evnoia Group. Within his umbrella of companies lies his most valued creation. Zero to Hero, LLC is a multi-faceted transformational education company. Zero to Hero focuses on producing highly impacting content for personal, educational, and community based strategies to improve performance.

Giving back is a huge part of his DNA. He enthusiastically designed and implemented an educational curriculum called "Alternative Pathways to Success" (APS). He recognized the future that lies in the hands of the children and their leadership capabilities. Personal development is a huge part of Reggie's make up. At the age of 19, he was exposed to information that helped chisel his character and personal philosophies. New concepts and profound information has made him the man he is today. He felt there was an exciting and innovative way to help transform our youth's belief system and thinking patterns by using APS as the solution. Reggie invested 3 days a week at Palmer Park Prep in Detroit, teaching 7th and 8th graders these life changing strategies. APS received rave reviews from teachers and students.

For More Information:

Reggie Flowers wants to lock arms with you!

For more information about training, products, programs, and live events, or to book Reggie for your next event, contact:

Zero to Hero, LLC
Troy, MI 48084
www.reggieflowers.com

References

<u>Jim Rohn</u> quotes – Building Your Network Marketing Business (audio)

<u>Earl Nightingale</u> quotes – The Strangest Secret – (audio)

<u>John Maxwell</u>- 15 Invaluable Laws of Growth. Publisher: Center Street (2012)

<u>Jay-Z</u> – Biography.com. retrieved 2016-11-08.

<u>J-Lo</u> - "Duty Captain's Report". *Court TV*. January 17, 2001. Archived from the original on February 9, 2008. Retrieved October 29, 2006. "Mamás y Mamacitas – Música". Terra Networks. May 11, 2007. Retrieved May 24, 2012.

<u>Michael Jordan</u> - Michael Jordan biography, <u>23jordan.com</u>. Retrieved November 23, 2007.

<u>Oprah Winfrey</u> –
- Jill Nelson, "The Man Who Saved Oprah Winfrey", *The Washington Post*, December 14, 1981; p. W30.
- "Ancestry of Oprah Winfrey". Genealogy.about.com. Retrieved 2014-08-22.
- Krohn, Katherine E, *Oprah Winfrey: Global Media Leader (USA Today)* (Krohn, 2002), ISBN 978-1-58013-571-9, p. 9.
- Jill Nelson. "The Man Who Saved Oprah Winfrey", *The Washington Post*, December 14, 1986, p. W30.
- Mair (1999) p. 12.
- Garson, Helen S. *Oprah Winfrey: A Biography* (Greenwood, 2004), ISBN 978-0-313-32339-3, p. 20.

- "Ancestry of Oprah Winfrey". Genealogy.about.com. Retrieved 2014-08-22.

Tyler Perry –
"Perry, Willie Maxine Campbell". *The Advocate*. December 11, 2009. Retrieved November 5, 2010.
"Willie Maxine Campbell Perry Obituary: View Willie Perry's Obituary by The Advocate". Legacy.com. December 8, 2009. Retrieved December 31, 2012.
"Tyler Perry Biography – Inspired by Oprah, Perseverance Paid Off, Concentrated on Madea Character". Net Industries. 2010. Retrieved January 16, 2010.
"Tyler Perry recounts childhood abuse on Web site". CNN. October 6, 2009.
Park, Michael Y. (October 6, 2009). "Tyler Perry Reveals He Was Abused as a Child". *People*. Retrieved January 20, 2010.

Napoleon Hill –
Hill, Napoleon (1937). Think and Grow Rich. Chicago, Illinois: Combined Registry Company. p. 8. ISBN 1-60506-930-2.

Tony Robbins -
Simon & Schuster Audio/Nightingale-Conant; Unabridged edition (May 8, 2012 ISBN-10: 1442352663).

Zig Ziglar –
Secrets of Closing the Sale (1984)

Lance Armstrong –
Biography.com Retrieved 2016-11-11.

Jack Canfield –
The Success Principals: How to Get from Where You Are to Where You Want to Be. ISBN-13: 9780060594893 HarperCollins Publishers; 12/26/2006

5 INCONTROVERTIBLE LAWS FOR SUCCESS

Engineered to Transform. Powered by Passion.

Congratulations!

I am honored that you've completed *The Art of the Struggle*. It is my prayer that you took the time to write down your vision, thoughts, and plans for your future. For doing the work, we are giving you a discount on my online course! If you enjoyed the book, you'll love comprehensive training on the 5 Incontrovertible Laws for Success.

The 5 Incontrovertible Laws for Success is the most effective transformational program for real people with real struggles. You will get:

- 5-week 5 Incontrovertible Laws for Success online training ($397 value)
- 15+ hours of training designed to fully immerse you in the 5 Laws
- Live Q & A coaching and monthly mentoring for 3 months ($297 value)
- Honoring the Struggle: a 3-part video roadmap series ($97 value)
- Signed certificate of completion ($29 value)
- World-class support (priceless)

That's a value of $820 and a customized strategy to help you get the desired results. But, you can receive an UNBELIEVABLE discount right now, with a 100%

satisfaction guarantee. Take advantage of your discount on our website: Reggieflowers.com Click on courses.

CPSIA information can be obtained
at www.ICGtesting.com
Printed in the USA
LVHW061255050120
642540LV00017BA/948/P